Homer's

ODYSSEY

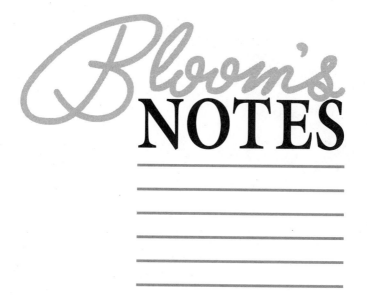

NOTES

Edited and with an Introduction by
HAROLD BLOOM

Printed and bound in the United States of America.

First Printing
1 3 5 7 9 8 6 4 2

ISBN 0-7910-3682-0

Chelsea House Publishers
1974 Sproul Road, Suite 400
P.O. Box 914
Broomall, PA 19008-0914

Contents

User's Guide

This volume is designed to present biographical, critical, and bibliographical information on Homer and the *Odyssey*. Following Harold Bloom's introduction, there appears a detailed biography of the author, discussing the major events in his life and his important literary works. Then follows a thematic and structural analysis of the work, in which significant themes, patterns, and motifs are traced. An annotated list of characters supplies brief information on the chief characters in the work.

A selection of critical extracts, derived from previously published material by leading critics, then follows. The extracts consist of such things as statements by the author on his work, early reviews of the work, and later evaluations down to the present day. The items are arranged chronologically by date of first publication. A bibliography of Homer (including important editions of the *Iliad* and *Odyssey* from the invention of printing to the present day, as well as selected English translations), a list of additional books and articles on him and on the *Odyssey,* and an index of themes conclude the volume.

Harold Bloom is Sterling Professor of the Humanities at Yale University and Henry W. and Albert A. Berg Professor of English at the New York University Graduate School. He is the author of twenty books and the editor of more than thirty anthologies of literature and literary criticism.

Professor Bloom's works include *Shelley's Mythmaking* (1959), *The Visionary Company* (1961), *Blake's Apocalypse* (1963), *Yeats* (1970), *A Map of Misreading* (1975), *Kabbalah and Criticism* (1975), and *Agon: Towards a Theory of Revisionism* (1982). *The Anxiety of Influence* (1973) sets forth Professor Bloom's provocative theory of the literary relationships between the great writers and their predecessors. His most recent books are *The American Religion* (1992) and *The Western Canon* (1994).

Professor Bloom earned his Ph.D. from Yale University in 1955 and has served on the Yale faculty since then. He is a 1985 MacArthur Foundation Award recipient and served as the Charles Eliot Norton Professor of Poetry at Harvard University in 1987–88. He is currently the editor of the Chelsea House series Major Literary Characters and Modern Critical Views, and other Chelsea House series in literary criticism.

Introduction

HAROLD BLOOM

Though an epic, the *Odyssey* has many attributes of the literary genre called the "romance," a marvelous story more inclined to fantasy than to realistic representation. Homer turns in the *Odyssey* to what might be defined as realistic descriptions of the marvelous, a formula apt for the hero Odysseus, who must avoid disasters as varied as being devoured by a one-eyed monster or drowning in freezing waters. The great burden for Odysseus is that his implacable enemy is Poseidon the sea god, and yet Odysseus is an island king who can get back to Ithaca only by passing through the realm of Poseidon. This immense difficulty can be surmounted only by a quester of endless resource: cunning, courageous, stubborn above all. The very name "Odysseus" (which became "Ulysses" in Latin) means either a curse's victim or an avenger who carries a curse to others. This ambiguity hints both at the sufferings of Odysseus and at his dangerousness to his enemies. He is a survivor: prudent, wise, perhaps a little cold. You do not want to be in one boat with him, however admirable you judge him to be: you may well drown, but he will reach land.

It has been argued that the *Odyssey,* for all its wonders, founds its storytelling upon the exclusion of surprise. That seems to me one of the prime aesthetic virtues of the poem: it insists upon working through its own suppositions, and so plays fair with the reader. Aristotle praised Homer for centering both his epics upon a single action, which in the *Odyssey* is the voyage home to Ithaca. The rugged simplicity of Homer's tale is its principal power; the story gives us a hero so skilled and tactful that he rarely abandons the long view. And yet the Odysseus who at last returns to his wife, son, and kingdom, is more than just two decades older and wiser than when he left; he is indeed a hero who has weathered archaic and magical adventures that are somehow at variance with his ultimate quest for simplicity. Odysseus has reemerged from a world that we identify as dreams and nightmares, and his embrace of an ordinary reality has in it a repudiation of fantasy as such. The hero has refused victimization by gods and by demons, and his triumph heartens the reader, who beholds in Odysseus an emblem of our heroic longing for the commonplace. Homer does not seem to reflect upon the irony that his hero finally refuses all enchantments even though the hero's very name indicates that Odysseus himself is an enchanter, a troublemaker for nearly everyone whom he ever encounters.

Many critics have seen Odysseus as the one figure in all literature who most uniquely establishes and sustains his own identity. Certainly, few characters in Western literature have so firm a conviction as to precisely how their identity is to be confirmed and renewed. Despite the wisdom of Odysseus, his identity is not easily maintained, since his great enemy is the ultimate shapeshifter, the god of all ocean. Athena, the hero's champion and guide, is well aware of the odds against Odysseus, and the hero himself knows how much he needs her assistance if he is to survive. His longing for return seems already an allegory for the soul's yearning, in Platonism and beyond, though Homer certainly did not see his Odysseus as a religious pilgrim. Ithaca, in the poem, means something realistic and simple, and yet going home, against the sea god's opposition, is bound to suggest transcendental elements as well.

Odysseus matures throughout the poem; he never suffers without learning from the experience, and his appeal to Athena may well be that he becomes more and more like her, except that he does not want to attain the detachment of the goddess, despite his own tendency to coldness and cunning when they seem essential for survival.

James Joyce thought that Odysseus was the one "complete" hero in literature and therefore chose Homer's voyager as the model for Leopold Bloom in *Ulysses*. Compared to Joyce's Bloom, who is a paradigm of kindness and sweetness, Homer's Odysseus is capable of great savagery, but this is never savagery for its own sake, nor will Odysseus resort to force until guile has failed him. The hero's comprehensiveness induces him to be pragmatic and to be concerned primarily with the question, Will it work? Americans therefore are likely to find something very American in Odysseus, even though our writers have yet to give us a convincing version of Homer's hero. The closest of all our literary characters to one aspect of Odysseus is Mark Twain's Huck Finn, whose innocent cunning sometimes suggests a childlike transformation of the Homeric hero into an American survivor. Perhaps all of American history is a closer analogue to the *Odyssey:* the American dream finally involves a hope of returning home, wiser and richer than when we departed from there in order to experience warfare, marvelous enchantments, and the forging of a self-reliant identity strong enough to bring us back to where we began. ✤

Biography of Homer

Homer (Homeros) is the reputed author of the two oldest epic poems of ancient Greece, the *Iliad* and the *Odyssey*. Even the Greeks, however, were uncertain of the very existence of Homer or of the time in which he lived, and it is now believed that, if there actually was a Homer, he did no more than organize or edit the poems roughly in the form in which they have come down to us.

In the 1930s Milman Parry discovered that the Homeric poems belonged to the tradition of oral poetry, in which long passages were committed to memory by bards or "rhapsodes" and recited in public assemblies or at the courts of kings or chieftains. Some parts of the Homeric poems—especially the *Iliad,* which is thought to be older than the *Odyssey*—probably predate the Trojan War (traditionally dated to 1184 B.C.E. but now dated by archaeological evidence to roughly 1220 B.C.E.). Conversely, other parts of the poems must date to a much later period. Homer probably brought the various sections of the two poems together no later than 700 B.C.E. All the works attributed to Homer are in an archaic form of the Ionic dialect of Greek, mostly spoken in what is now western Turkey.

Seven cities in Greece, both on the mainland and on some of the islands in the Aegean Sea, claimed the honor of being the birthplace of Homer. The conventional belief that he was blind rests largely upon a passage in the so-called *Homeric Hymns,* a series of thirty-three poems celebrating the gods of the Greek pantheon. Many rhapsodes, however, were in fact blind.

The *Iliad* and the *Odyssey* are each unified in themselves, although they are very different from each other in tone and subject matter. The *Iliad* deals with the final stages of the Trojan War between the Greeks and the Trojans, and most of the action takes place in the Troad (a region in northwestern Turkey). The ostensible cause of the war is the abduction of Helen (the wife of Menelaus) by Alexandros (or Paris); but the *Iliad* focuses largely on the personal battle between the Greek Achilles and the Trojan Hector. Although much of the poem is taken up with battles, there is a lofty, aristocratic character to the *Iliad* that may reflect the attitudes of the nobility prior to the classical age of Greek civilization. The poem is resolved when Achilles defeats Hector in single combat and, after dragging his body around the walls of Troy in triumph, hands it over to Hector's father Priam.

The events in the *Iliad* are not, of course, likely to be a literal account of an historical event. Although there probably was something corresponding to the Trojan War, it now seems clear that the war was waged not between two groups of racially or ethnically distinct peoples (Greeks and Trojans) but between two factions of early Greeks, called Mycenaeans, who flourished in the second millennium B.C.E. The cause of the war may have been a dispute over the control of the Hellespont, the narrow channel leading to the Black Sea.

It is believed by many that the *Odyssey* was assembled at a much later date than the *Iliad,* since it seems to reflect a greater knowledge of the Mediterranean world as gained by the Greeks in their colonizing and trading ventures in the ninth and eighth centuries B.C.E. The *Odyssey* is an adventure story about the wanderings of Odysseus after the Trojan War. His travels take him as far west as the islands of the Hesperides (perhaps a reference to Gibraltar) and even to the Greek underworld, where he meets the souls of the dead. Eventually Odysseus returns home to the small island of Ithaca (off the western coast of Greece), defeats the suitors who have been vainly courting his wife, Penelope, for twenty years, and reunites with her and with his son, Telemachus.

Several other works were attributed by the Greeks either to Homer or to the *Homeridae* ("the sons of Homer"). These include the Trojan Cycle (a group of six epic poems—most now surviving only in fragments—dealing with other aspects of the Trojan War than were covered by Homer), the *Homeric Hymns,* and three burlesques or parodies: the *Margites;* the *Cercopes* ("Monkey-Men"); and the *Batrachomyomachia* ("Battle of the Frogs and Mice"). The first two of these parodies exist only in brief fragments. All these poems were written considerably later than the *Iliad* and *Odyssey,* dating from the seventh to the fifth centuries B.C.E.

The Homeric poems were, in essence, the Bible of the Greeks. They incorporated much of what was believed about the gods (Zeus, Hera, Athena, Apollo, Hermes, and many others), who were thought to dwell on the top of Mount Olympus in northeastern Greece. Although Homer was an immense influence on subsequent Greek literature, the respect with which he and his work were held is reflected by the fact that no later poet in Greece or Rome ever retold the stories of Achilles and Hector or of Odysseus, even though most of the other legends about the Greek gods and heroes were retold many times by poets, dramatists, and historians.

The *Iliad* and the *Odyssey* were each divided into twenty-four books in the third century B.C.E. At this time the Greeks began to lay the groundwork for later scholarship and criticism by determining the proper text of the poems (certain portions were deemed spurious or the work of later interpolators) and by writing commentaries elucidating the poems. An important commentary was written by the scholar Aristarchus (c. 216–c. 144 B.C.E.), large fragments of which survive.

Homer was tremendously influential on Latin literature as well. His greatest disciple was Vergil (P. Vergilius Maro), who toward the end of the first century B.C.E. wrote the *Aeneid,* an epic poem consciously based upon the *Iliad* and the *Odyssey* telling the tale of the wanderings of Aeneas (a minor figure mentioned in the *Iliad*) from Troy to Italy. The Romans referred to Odysseus as Ulixes or Ulysses.

The influence of the Homeric poems upon Western literature has been incalculable; it can be sensed from works as diverse as Dante's *Divine Comedy* to James Joyce's *Ulysses* (1922). The modern Greek poet Nikos Kazantzakis wrote a sequel to the *Odyssey* under the title *Odysseia* (1938; translated into English in 1958 as *The Odyssey: A Modern Sequel*).

Homer's works were among the earliest to be published when printing was invented in the mid-fifteenth century. The work of many scholars has now established the Greek text of Homer on as sound a basis as possible, and many helpful commentaries have been written, notably by W. B. Stanford (1947–48).

The Homeric poems were first translated into English by the poet George Chapman in 1616. Since then, many distinguished writers have published translations, from Thomas Hobbes to Alexander Pope to William Cullen Bryant to William Morris to Robert Fitzgerald. Some of these translations have been in prose, including those by S. H. Butcher and Andrew Lang, Samuel Butler, T. E. Shaw (T. E. Lawrence), and E. V. Rieu. The translation of the *Odyssey* by the classical scholar Richmond Lattimore attempts a line-for-line translation and perhaps captures the flavor of the Greek original better than many others. ❖

Thematic and Structural Analysis

Along with its companion, the *Iliad,* and some of the writings in the Old Testament, the *Odyssey* is among the oldest works of Western literature. Indeed, it is hard to be sure exactly how old it is. Most scholars agree that it was written down in something close to its current form during the eighth century B.C.E. by a Greek-speaking poet conventionally called Homer. But there is also a general consensus that Homer did not himself invent the characters and incidents of the poem but rather organized and recorded a set of stories that had been sung by wandering bards for countless generations. The poem's roots in an oral tradition are suggested by some of the stylistic features that modern readers find most odd, such as repeated epithets ("gray-eyed Athena" or "rosy-fingered Dawn"). It is now believed that these repeated phrases and some of the longer formulaic passages in the poem were probably used as reference points by which singers would orient themselves as they performed. In general, it is helpful in reading the *Odyssey* to keep in mind that it was not so much the inspired production of a singular poet as it was the distillation of the long-accumulated lore and wisdom of an archaic culture. The values of this culture have been handed down to our own culture through the writings of Plato and Aristotle, the Greek tragedians, and the many medieval, Renaissance, and modern writers who were educated in the classical tradition.

At the core of the value system of the *Odyssey* is a certain conception of moral virtue and human excellence. This conception is embodied in the larger-than-life central figure of the poem—Odysseus. Odysseus is a "hero" in the purest sense of the term.

He is presented to us not as a flawed human being like ourselves, but as a model of righteous and admirable behavior. He possesses in abundance virtually all the qualities that made human life noble, dignified, and beautiful in the eyes of the ancient Greeks. He is exceptionally crafty and intelligent, as we see in the story of the Trojan horse or when he outsmarts the Cyclops. He is physically powerful and athletic, as we see when he strings the bow that none of the suitors could handle or hurls a discus further than any of the Phaeacians. He is a brave and nearly invincible warrior, as we see when he almost single-handedly destroys more than a hundred suitors in one sustained fight. He is extremely eloquent in his speech and, perhaps more important, knows the right thing to say in formal social situations. He has in general a highly refined sense of courtesy, propriety, and respect for custom. He is intensely loyal to his family, friends, and homeland. He is patient and persevering and has deep reverence for the gods. But unlike for Christian heroes, Odysseus' reward for his many virtues is not delayed until an afterlife. Odysseus is not expected to stand passively by and accept his just deserts in heaven. On the contrary, the principal motivation behind his moral and martial vigor is the material wealth, political authority, and, most important to the Greeks, widespread honor and fame it helps him to win.

In fact, Odysseus has already won all these things to a certain degree before the story of the *Odyssey* begins. He has established himself as the preeminent nobleman on his home island of Ithaca. He is the head of a sumptuous household and commands the labor of many servants. He has ample stores of treasure and gifts gained from raids and other travels. He is the proud husband of a coveted bride, Penelope, and the father of a promising son, Telemachus. He leaves Ithaca to join a host of other Greek noblemen in battle against the Trojans, and his performance as a warrior and strategist in this ten-year struggle, as related in the *Iliad,* has confirmed his reputation for great valor and exceptional cunning. On the way home from this long war, however, Odysseus manages unintentionally to offend Poseidon, and in revenge the ocean god puts Odysseus through an extended series of very severe tests before allowing him to come home. The story of this ordeal provides one of the two connected narratives that make up the substance of the *Odyssey.* The other is the story of the difficulties encountered by Odysseus' son and wife, Telemachus and Penelope, as they attempt to maintain control over his household during his long absence. The two strains are joined toward the conclusion of the book when Odysseus does finally return and joins with his son and his few loyal servants to restore order to his home.

The focus as the poem starts is not on Odysseus but on his son. Telemachus' coming of age, his passing from adolescence to full manhood, is perhaps the most important secondary theme of the poem. This process is dramatized most vividly in the **first four books** as we see Telemachus begin to take a more active and assertive role in establishing order in his father's house. We first see him through the eyes of Odysseus' divine protector, Athena, as she descends on Ithaca and takes the form of Mentes, a former fighting companion of the absent hero. She enters Odysseus' home, where she finds a large number of men behaving loosely, lounging about, playing draughts, eating meat in large quantities, and joking among themselves. Telemachus sits apart, nursing grim thoughts about what his father might do to these crass men if he were suddenly to return. Athena/Mentes approaches and attempts to rouse Telemachus out of his sullen passivity. She tells him that she believes Odysseus is still alive, and she predicts that he will soon return to Ithaca. When the gathered men begin to dance and sing raucously, she asks, "What feast is this? A serious man could well be scandalized, seeing such disgraceful behaviour." Telemachus replies that many of the men are suitors for his mother's hand in marriage. In his father's absence, he explains, they gather at his house, eat his food, and use up his wealth as they wait for Penelope to make a decision about which of them she favors. She has delayed them for years by neither accepting nor refusing their offers, Telemachus relates, but they are now becoming increasingly insistent that she make a choice.

Greatly indignant, Mentes/Athena advises Telemachus about how to get rid of the suitors. Tell them to go back to their own homes, she says, and then prepare a ship and sail to Pylos and question Nestor, one of Odysseus' fighting companions in the Trojan War, about the great warrior's whereabouts. From there, proceed to Sparta and question his brother-in-arms Menelaus as well. If you find out Odysseus is alive, she says, stay away for another year before returning. If you find out he is dead, come home, pile up a tomb in his honor, and make great sacrifices to the gods, "as is fitting." Then give your mother to a husband and make a plan to kill the rest of the suitors. "You should not go on clinging to your childhood," Athena/Mentes concludes. "Since I can see you are big and splendid, be bold also, so that in generations to come they will praise you." Sensing that Mentes is a god in disguise, Telemachus is emboldened and energized by these words. When Penelope comes down the stairs to ask the singer not to sing "sad songs" about Troy, Telemachus addresses her with a forceful- ness that surprises his mother. The suitors are no less surprised when the formerly sullen boy speaks up confidently and demands their presence at an assembly the following morning. There, he says, he will give them his "forthright statement," insisting that they go elsewhere lest he call upon Zeus, asking "that you may perish in this house, with no payment given."

At the assembly the next day (**book two**), Telemachus is no less self-possessed. Athena puts an "enchantment of grace" upon him, so that as he sits in his father's seat before the assembled male citizens of Ithaca he appears impressive and imposing. He speaks eloquently of the grief of losing his father and of the scandal caused by the suitors. "No longer are the things endurable that have been done," he says, calling upon the parasitical young nobles to leave his father's house. The chief among them, Antinoos, replies by shifting the blame on to Penelope. He complains that she makes promises to each man but never fulfills any of them. And he tells the now- famous story of how Penelope delayed by telling the suitors that she could not make a decision until she had completed weaving a shroud for the hero Laertes, Odysseus' father. She would weave the shroud by day, he explains, but then by night she secretly would undo everything she had done. She kept up this stratagem for three years before it was discovered, but now they have forced her to finish. Antinoos vows that he and his friends will not go back to their own estates until Penelope marries whichever Achaean she fancies. Telemachus refuses to take the suitors' side against his mother, and he vows again that if these idle young men continue to eat him out of house and home he will call upon Zeus to grant a reversal of fortunes. He tells the assembly of his intention to go to Pylos and Sparta to try to find news of his father. Only if he finds out that his father is dead will he ask his mother to decide on a new husband. The suitors are again impressed by Telemachus' newfound eloquence and resolve. Back in the house after the assembly has broken up, Antinoos tries to soften Telemachus up a bit by offering to drink with him. But Telemachus makes it clear that his feelings can no longer be suppressed. "The anger is steaming up inside me," he says ominously, and goes to the storerooms to prepare for his journey.

Telemachus comes further into his own during the time he spends at Pylos and Sparta in **books three and four**. He is initially bashful before the eminent old warriors Nestor and Menelaus, but with Athena's help he quickly becomes adept at the formalities and courtesies of adult friendship. The relationship between guests and hosts was a matter of the greatest importance in the culture for which the *Odyssey* was written. Because it was a clannish world in which outsiders were usually regarded with much suspicion and hostility, an elaborate set of conventions had developed to govern their behavior and their treatment. The *Odyssey* may well have functioned in part as a manual for how to conduct oneself in guest-host situations. Telemachus' mastery of these delicate conventions is a sign of his newfound maturity. Both Nestor and Menelaus respond warmly to his overtures, sharing his outrage about the suitors, treating him to their finest food and drink, entertaining him, and offering him generous gifts and almost unlimited assistance. They also both tell him everything they know about the fate of Odysseus. In Nestor's case, this is not very much. He recalls the long struggles and sorrows of the Trojan War and confirms Odysseus' reputation for shrewdness and guile. But after parting company with Odysseus on the way home from the war, Nestor has neither seen him nor heard much trustworthy news.

Menelaus, on the other hand, has much to report. Along with his wife, Helen, he also recalls Odysseus' extraordinary feats of cunning during the war. Helen tells of the time when Odysseus gained entrance into Troy by disguising himself as a beggar, striking down many Trojans and gaining much valuable information. (The story foreshadows Odysseus' return to Ithaca, when he enters his own house disguised as a beggar.)

Menelaus tells the famous story of the Trojan horse, confirming for Telemachus the greatness of his father. "Nowhere have I seen with my own eyes anything like him, nor known an inward heart like the heart of enduring Odysseus." More important, Menelaus assures Telemachus that Odysseus is alive. He learned this from no less a source than Proteus, "the old man of the sea." In an effort to get off of the island of Paphos, where he found himself stranded after the Trojan War, Menelaus explains how he had disguised himself as one of Proteus' flock of seals and then caught him in his grasp, holding on while the mutable god transformed himself into every natural beast and form. When Proteus finally tired and asked Menelaus his purpose, he requested to be told which god was preventing him from leaving the island and what had been the fate of his fellow Achaeans. Odysseus, Proteus told Menelaus, was stuck on the island of Calypso, alive and whole, but with no men and no ship and thus no means of escaping this lustful nymph.

This is the condition in which we first encounter Odysseus in **book five**. After Telemachus leaves Menelaus, and we see the suitors preparing to ambush the young man on his return to Ithaca, our attention is at last turned to the hero himself. We find him sitting outside of Calypso's cave, weeping bitterly— "breaking his heart in tears, lamentation, and sorrow." To be a hero and therefore above ordinary human weaknesses was not by any means to be above ordinary human suffering. On the contrary, the depth and persistence of the emotional pain that Odysseus endures and overcomes is an important part of his greatness. A mood of sorrow, loss, and longing pervades the poem from the beginning. It is part of the effect of starting the poem with Telemachus and Penelope; their sense of absence and disruption carries through the entire story. We repeatedly see Odysseus weeping, at times out of remorse for lost companions, at times out of nostalgia for past glories, at times out of homesickness, and at times out of sheer vexation at the difficulties the gods put in his way. "The inward heart was broken within him," the poet often says. The pain is only finally relieved when Odysseus rejoins his family, kills the suitors, and rewards his few loyal servants. But before he can do this he first must somehow escape from Calypso's island, where he has now been stranded for seven years.

As is often the case, Odysseus' escape is only made possible by Athena's helpful intervention. She persuades Zeus to take pity on the wretched mortal, and he in turn sends Hermes to instruct Calypso to let Odysseus leave. Reluctantly bowing to the will of the greatest of the gods, Calypso allows Odysseus to build a raft and gives him a supply of food and wine, but she refuses to help him any further. Assuring the suspicious hero that she is not playing a trick on him, she tells him that he would not wish to go if he knew the troubles that were in store for him. But Odysseus is characteristically resolute. He acknowledges that Calypso is more beautiful than Penelope—"She is mortal after all, and you are immortal and ageless"—but he has fought too hard to give up now:

> What I want and all my days I pine for
> is to go back to my house and see my day of homecoming.
> And if some god batters me far out on the wine-blue water,
> I will endure it, keeping a stubborn spirit inside me,
> For already I have suffered much and done much hard work
> on the waves and in the fighting. So let this adventure follow.

He sets out bravely, and after seventeen days of sailing on the open ocean he spots the mountains of the island of Phaeacia. Poseidon is not about to let him land troublefree, however, so he kicks up a storm. Odysseus sees it coming and wishes he had died a glorious death in Troy rather than a dismal one at sea. He is soon tossed from the raft, which is then shattered by the force of the waves. But he hangs on to a splinter, and with the help of Athena and the nymph Leukothea, after two further days and nights he makes it wearily ashore. There, in **book six,** he is found by the princess Nausicaa, who is initially frightened of him but, with the aid of Athena, overcomes her fear and receives him kindly.

Phaeacia, as depicted in **book seven**, is a utopia. Ruled by a wise king, Alcinoos, and a virtuous queen, Arete, it is the one place Odysseus visits on his many travels where harmony and order seem to prevail. The king and queen live in a splendid palace, with golden and silver carvings by Hephaestus, the smithy god, on the lintels. It is surrounded by magnificent orchards and vineyards. "Never is the fruit spoiled on these," the poet tells us, "never does it give out." Odysseus' eloquence, good manners, and impressive appearance soon convince the Phaeacians that he is no ordinary wayfarer. He is treated courteously and generously, as befits a guest of high stature. The Phaeacians promise to take him home on their ships, and in the meantime he is fed, given a place to sleep, and invited to participate in athletic contests performed before Alcinoos and Arete. After he excels in these games (**book eight**), Odysseus asks for a demonstration of the Phaeacians' famed skill in dancing, and they magnificently comply. Finally, a blind singer by the name of Demodocos (perhaps a figure for Homer himself) is brought in. Odysseus tells him that he honors singers (poets) "above all mortals," and he asks him to tell the story of the Trojan horse. Odysseus weeps as he hears the story of his own guile, and Alcinoos begins to suspect that his guest is of a high stature indeed. He calls upon Odysseus to identify himself: "Tell me the name by which your mother and father called you. . . . Tell me your land, your neighborhood, and your city. . . . Where were you drawn off course, what countries peopled by men did you come to . . .? Which [men] were savage and violent and without justice, which were hospitable and godly?"

Odysseus' answer to these questions forms the most famous part of the *Odyssey*. In a section of four books (**nine through twelve**) known as "The Great Wanderings," Odysseus tells the Phaeacians the story of the many adventures and misfortunes that befell him between the end of the Trojan War and his captivity on Calypso's island. The story follows the pattern of a trial by ordeal, in which Odysseus is subjected to a broad range of tests of his courage, cleverness, skill, and endurance. His knowledge of the world is expanded at every stage as he encounters a wide variety of divine, human, and subhuman peoples and civilizations. Perhaps the most important lesson that is repeatedly brought home to him is that of moderation, or due respect for the limits that distinguish the merely human from the divine. The primary reason that he alone survives the ordeal of the wanderings while all his men perish is that he most unfailingly honors the warnings and instructions of the gods. (Aristotle, with frequent reference to Homeric heroes such as Odysseus, would later rank prudence—the awareness of limitations and the capacity to look ahead with caution—first among the virtues.)

The first of the many strange peoples Odysseus encounters after departing from Troy are the Ciconians, who live on the island of Ismaros (**book nine**). Things start out well here, as Odysseus and his men successfully sack their city and gain much treasure. But the men do not take Odysseus' advice to leave quickly after the battle. Instead, they stay, get drunk, and slay many sheep and oxen. The Ciconians take this opportunity to gather reinforcements, and they return and rout Odysseus' men, killing six from each ship. The rest flee, grieving for their lost companions. It is the first of many occasions when a prideful lack of prudence on the part of Odysseus' men has disastrous results.

After nine days at sea, the ships come upon the island of the Lotus-Eaters. These people are peaceful enough, spending their days in a kind of drug-induced haze. But they introduce some of the men to the soporific "honey-sweet fruit" of the lotus plant, which causes them to forget about their homes and their mission. Odysseus must forcibly remove them from the balmy island and return them to the labor of the ship. Again the men are nearly done in by a desire to escape the pain and difficulty of ordinary human existence.

They soon wish they were back with the Lotus-Eaters, however, when they find themselves at odds with the brutal giant Polyphemus, one of a race of beings called Cyclopes ("one-eyed men"). Odysseus has taken twelve of the best men ashore with him to investigate the nature of the "monster-like" men they have seen from the ship. He carries with him a goatskin full of exceptionally potent sweet wine that had been given to him by a priest of Apollo. Against the cautionary advice of his companions, Odysseus enters the cave of Polyphemus. The huge man enters soon afterward, rolling an immense stone in front of the entrance. "Strangers, who are you?" he asks, after methodically milking his goats. Odysseus speaks up in reply, identifying the group as wayfarers. He invokes Zeus and asks the honors due to suppliants and guests. Polyphemus laughs at the invocation, saying he has no fear of the gods, and proceeds to pick up two of Odysseus' men, dash their brains on the floor, cut them up, and eat them. He then lays down to sleep. Odysseus considers stabbing the monster in his sleep, but with characteristic foresight he realizes that he and his men would then be trapped in the cave, because they would be unable to remove the stone from in front of the entrance. They wait in terror until the next day, when once again the Cyclops eats two men before going out of the cave. While he is gone, Odysseus and his men take a long piece of wood from the monster's store, shave one end of it to a sharp point, and harden the tip in the fire. When the Cyclops returns and devours two more men, Odysseus offers him a drink from his sack of wine. The monster accepts, drinking heartily three times from the potent brew, and asks Odysseus his name. Odysseus tells him his name is Outis ("nobody"). The monster replies pitilessly that in return for his generous gift of wine, he will be eaten after his friends. He then falls into a drunken sleep, gurgling up vomit of human flesh. Odysseus and his men twist the post into his single eye, and Polyphemus awakens, screaming out for the other Cyclopes to come and help him. His fellow monsters gather around outside of the cave and ask him who is doing him harm. "Nobody!" he replies. "Nobody is killing me by treachery!" Reassured, the other Cyclopes go away. Polyphemus then rolls away the boulder and sits in the entrance, waiting for anyone to try to escape. Odysseus outsmarts him again, however, by advising each of his men to cling to the underside of one of the Cyclops' goats. The monster checks the backs of the goats but neglects to check underneath them, so when they go out to pasture they carry Odysseus and his men to freedom. Odysseus yells out and taunts the Cyclops from his ship as they sail away from the island. The monster hurls enormous rocks at the sound of the voice and nearly destroys the ship. More damaging, he calls upon his father, Poseidon, to take revenge upon these travelers.

Poseidon's anger is slow to awaken, however, and the travelers fare better, at first, at the next island (**book ten**). Aeolus, the god of the winds, treats them courteously. When they leave, he tries to help them by giving Odysseus an ox-skin bag tied up with silver, which contains "the four winds." Odysseus stores it in the hollow of the boat, and ten nights later he and his men come within view of the land of their fathers. But envious of Odysseus' gifts, his men decide while Odysseus is sleeping to find out how much gold is contained in the ox-skin bag. They open it and the released winds carry the ships far away from their home once again. When Odysseus awakens, he nearly despairs. "I waking pondered deeply in my own blameless spirit, whether to throw myself over the side and die on the open water, or wait it out in silence, and still be one of the living." Choosing to stay among the living, he takes the ships back to the island of Aeolus. He explains what happened and asks for help again. But Aeolus rejects him and sends him away, suspecting that for a man to have such bad luck he "must be hateful to the immortals."

Their next encounter seems to bear this out, as every ship except that of Odysseus is destroyed by a huge army of man-eating Laestrygonians. These giants gather at the shore of their island and spear Odysseus' men like so many fish, carrying then away for feasting. The lone remaining ship then limps into the harbor of an island by the name of Aeaea. Odysseus and his men stay in the harbor for two days, "eating [their] hearts out" for their lost companions. Venturing ashore, they then divide themselves into two parties, one led by Odysseus and one led by Eurylachus. Eurylachus' party is chosen by lot to investigate smoke they see rising from the trees a short distance away. They find a house with a beautiful goddess by the name of Circe weaving at a loom and singing beautifully. She invites them to dine with her and gives them a potion that changes their heads and mouths into those of pigs. Although they still have human intelligence, they are locked into a pig-pen and fed pig's food. Eurylachus manages to escape without drinking the potion and returns to tell Odysseus of this terrible occurrence. Odysseus straps on his sword and sets out toward the house of the goddess. On the way, Hermes appears to him in the guise of a young man and gives him a medicine called moly which will render him immune to Circe's potion. He is instructed to draw his sword and approach her as if to kill her as soon as she touches him with his wand. She will be frightened and offer to sleep with you, Hermes tells Odysseus. Do not refuse her, he says, but make her promise that she has no further plan against you, and that she will take care of you and your companions. Things play out more or less exactly as Hermes predicts; the men are changed back from pigs to men, Odysseus sleeps with Circe, and she takes generous care of the entire crew for months on end. After a year has passed the men become restless, and Circe instructs Odysseus that in order to make it home at last he must first journey to the land of the dead and consult the prophet Teiresias. His heart once again breaking within him, Odysseus sets out with his small group of surviving companions. Unwittingly, they leave behind Elpenor, drunk and asleep on the roof of Circe's house. He rolls off and breaks his neck soon after their departure.

Arriving at the foggy and cloud-hidden island of the Cimmerian people, Odysseus goes to the place of which Circe had told him and follows her instructions to the letter. Soon he finds himself approached by the spirits of the dead (**book eleven**). First among them is Elpenor, who explains how he died and asks to be properly buried. Odysseus promises to do so. The next to approach is Anticlea, Odysseus' mother, who was alive when he left for Troy. But for all his sorrow upon seeing her, Odysseus remembers Circe's instructions and will not let her come too close until he has questioned Teiresias. Teiresias then approaches and explains to Odysseus that it will be very difficult for him to make it back to Ithaca because Poseidon will punish him for blinding his son. Even so, the prophet says, you might still make it if "you can contain your own desire and your companions, when you first arrive at the island of Thrinacia, and find the cattle of Helios." If these cattle are harmed, Teiresias warns, Odysseus' ship and companions will be destroyed. Odysseus himself may get away, but even so he will come home without companions, in someone else's ship, and he will find troubles in his household, with insolent men eating away his livelihood and courting his wife. Odysseus' mother is then allowed to come forward, and in one of the most poignant exchanges of the poem she asks her son how he came there. He explains how and then asks her the same question. She tells him that she died of grief during his long absence: "It was my longing for you, your cleverness and your gentle ways, that took the sweet spirit of life from me."

Odysseus tries to embrace his mother three times, but each time she passes through his arms, "like a shadow or a dream." "Mother, why will you not wait for me?" Odysseus asks. Her reply speaks of the absolute limit that all human beings must ultimately accept: "The sinews no longer hold the flesh and the bones together."

After his mother's spirit departs, a number of other souls speak to Odysseus. First come many queens of the past who approach one by one and tell Odysseus their story. Then comes Agamemnon, who tells Odysseus of his death at the hands of Aegisthus and his own "sluttish" wife, Clytemnestra. He compliments Odysseus on the virtuousness of Penelope and advises him to arrive home secretly. The souls of Achilles and other heroes from the war, such as Patroclus, Antilochus, and Ajax, then draw near. Odysseus tells Achilles that even among the dead he is honored. But the greatest of the Greek heroes rejects Odysseus' effort at consolation with famous words that articulate emphatically the Greeks' pre-Christian emphasis on this world rather than the next. "Never try to console me for dying," Achilleus says. "I would rather follow the plough as thrall to another man, than be king over all the perished dead." Only Odysseus' words about the valor and virtuousness of Achilles's son give the unhappy shade any relief. When Achilles walks away, all the rest of the souls of the perished gather close to Odysseus, each one speaking in turn and telling of his sorrows.

Upon leaving the underworld in **book twelve**, Odysseus immediately fulfills his promise to the shade of Elpenor by returning to Circe's island and giving his body a proper burial. Circe then gives him extensive advice about the next stage of his long journey. First, she warns him, you will encounter the "strong enchantment" of the Sirens, whose beautiful singing is irresistible to mortal ears. They will entrap you eternally, she says, unless you stop your companions' ears with melted honey and have yourself lashed to the mast "so that you can hear, but not succumb." She then advises him how to pass through the "Rovers"—great rocks upon whose sides many ships have been shattered because the sea makes it impossible to determine their precise location. If these are successfully negotiated, Circe continues, you must then pass between Scylla and Charybdis, the former a ghastly monster with twelve feet, twelve hands, and six heads, and the latter a vast whirlpool that three times a day sucks a great expanse of water into a whirling vortex. She advises Odysseus to avoid Charybdis and pass by Scylla, because it is better to lose six men than one's entire ship and all one's companions. Only then, she says, will you and your men reach Thrinacia, where are pastured the beautiful cattle of Helios. Only if these cattle are unharmed, she warns, will you be allowed to continue on to your homes in Ithaca.

All happens as Circe foretells, including the death of six men at the hands of Scylla—"the most pitiful scene these eyes have looked on in my sufferings," Odysseus relates, "as I explored the routes over the water." But after the survivors arrive on Thrinacia, the winds cease to blow and they are stranded for many days without food. Nearing starvation, the men give in. In Odysseus' absence, they slaughter and eat the cattle of the god. In revenge, Zeus sinks their ship in a storm soon after their departure from the island. Only Odysseus survives, hanging on to the broken keel and mast for nine days until he is carried to Ogygia, the island home of Calypso.

At this point (**book thirteen**), Odysseus concludes his long narration to the Phaeacians, saying that the rest has already been told. The great hall is "stricken to silence" as Odysseus finishes. Alcinoos speaks up first and promises that Odysseus will not now lose his homecoming after having endured so much suffering. The Phaeacians give him many generous gifts, and the next day they feast and take him aboard ship. He sleeps throughout the entire journey—"the gentlest and sweetest kind of sleep with no awakening." He continues to sleep when they arrive at Ithaca, so the Phaiakians carry him quietly on to the shore of his homeland and leave him under an olive tree with his many possessions. He does not recognize Ithaka when he first awakens because Athena has placed a mist over it that disguises its features. He laments that he has come to yet another strange land and curses the Phaeacians for leaving him there when they said they would take him home. Athena soon appears in the form of a young shepherd boy, however, and tells him that this is Ithaca. Odysseus is perplexed and delighted, but he hides his feelings, saying only that he had heard of such a place when he was in Crete. Athena then changes herself into a tall and beautiful woman, and she tells Odysseus who she really is. She praises him for his cleverness and tells him she has come to help him hide his possessions and to prepare for the difficulties he now must endure. But Odysseus still does not believe her. Again she speaks admiringly of his wariness and reason, and then clears away the mist, revealing the familiar landscape. Odysseus rejoices and kisses the ground. He sits with the goddess under the olive tree and they plan the destruction of the suitors. Athena departs to bring Telemachus back from Argos, and Odysseus, dressed as a beggar, walks inland toward the home of a swineherd, one of his former servants.

At the beginning of **book fourteen** Eumaeus, the swineherd, does not recognize his former master in his beggar's disguise but nonetheless treats him kindly and generously. The hero tests his former servant's loyalty several times, and in every instance the humble man responds correctly—expressing rage at the behavior of the suitors and great affection for his long-absent master, whom he believes to be dead. Odysseus is impressed both by the obvious sincerity of Eumaeus' words and by the graciousness of his behavior to the mere beggar he believes Odysseus to be. When later they sit and exchange stories (**book fifteen**), he finds out that Eumaeus was actually the son of a king but was stolen as a child and given to the Phoenicians, who left him off at Ithaca, where Laertes bought him. For his part, Eumaeus is skeptical about the stories of the beggar/Odysseus, especially his assurances that Odysseus is alive and will return soon. Every wayfarer tries to get the ear of Penelope by making up such stories, the swineherd snorts. He is still ignorant of the identity of his guest when Telemachus arrives the next day and sends him to tell Penelope and Laertes that he has evaded the ambush of the suitors and arrived home safely. Like Eumaeus, Telemachus treats the beggar/Odysseus graciously. But unlike Eumaeus, Telemachus is not left in ignorance for very long. Eager to begin his vengeance on the suitors, Odysseus quickly reveals his true identity to his son (**book sixteen**). They embrace, sit down together, and weep; "the desire for mourning rose in both of them." But they do not indulge their emotions for too long. They turn quickly to making plans to revenge themselves upon the suitors.

Odysseus' strategy is a characteristically effective mixture of subterfuge, faith in the gods, and heroic force. He and Telemachus return separately to Odysseus' house (**book seventeen**). Still dressed as a beggar, Odysseus spends two days cadging food from the suitors and absorbing their taunts and blows. Even when one throws a stool at him, he does not betray his disguise. He secretly instructs Telemachus to remove all the weapons except for two sets of armor and four spears from their place in the main hall, on the excuse that he wants to protect them from the smoke of the cooking fires. He learns which of his servants beside Eumaeus has remained faithful— only an old nurse, Eurycleia, who nearly gives him away when she recognizes a scar on his leg (**book nineteen**), and Philoetius, a goatherd. He also learns from Penelope that she is planning on the following day to sponsor a contest for her hand. Still believing he is a transient beggar, she confesses to him that she will bring down the great bow of Odysseus the following day. Whichever of the suitors is able to string it and shoot an arrow through a line of twelve axes will have the right to marry her.

The next day, Odysseus reveals his true identity in private to Eumaeus and Philoetius (**book twenty**). He tells Eumaeus to bring him the bow when he calls for it and then to lock the doors to the house. He tells Philoetius to lock the doors of the courtyard at the same time. The suitors soon gather with their usual drinking and cavorting, and Penelope comes down and announces her contest. One by one they fail even to string Odysseus' bow (**book twenty-one**). Still disguised, Odysseus calls for the bow, and Eumaeus carries it to him, against the wishes of the suitors. Odysseus strings it with ease and shoots an arrow through the twelve axes. He then strips off his rags, leaps to the threshold, and shoots an arrow through the neck of Antinoos, the leader of the suitors. Telemachus retrieves the spears and the armor and comes to his side. Athena lends a hand in the battle that ensues, and all the suitors are destroyed (**book twenty-two**).

In conclusion, Odysseus cleans his household with sulphur—an act symbolic of the restoration of propriety and order. He gives his loyal servants lands and titles. He is then blissfully reunited with his wife, Penelope, and his father, Laertes (**books twenty-three and twenty-four**). All is not perfectly settled, however. Odysseus explains to Penelope that according to the prophecy of Teiresias, he now must journey to a distant place where the people have never seen ships or seafaring men. He must carry his oar on his shoulder until one who sees it thinks it is a winnowing fan. There he must plant the oar in the ground and offer hecatombs to Poseidon. It will then be certain that "Death will come to me from the sea, in some altogether unwarlike way, and it will end me in the ebbing time of a sleek old age. My people about me will prosper." Penelope accepts that one last journey is necessary, and the three generations of heroes—Laertes, Odysseus, and Telemachus—join together to defeat the vengeful families of the suitors. ❖

—Neil Dolan
Harvard University

List of Characters

Odysseus is the hero of the *Odyssey*. His efforts to reach his home in Ithaca after the Trojan War form the central focus of the poem. He embodies many of the qualities most admired in ancient Greek culture—intelligence, prudence, courage, strength in battle, agility in athletics, and, most distinctively, wiliness or guile.

Telemachus is the loyal son of Odysseus. After suffering for many years the abuses of the suitors in the absence of his father, he comes into his maturity at the beginning of the poem and takes an active role in ousting them.

Penelope is Odysseus' devoted wife. During her husband's ten-year absence, she delays the many suitors for her hand by saying she cannot remarry until she has finished weaving a shroud for the aging father of her husband. She weaves by day and undoes her work by night. She is ultimately rewarded for her patience and cleverness by the return of her husband and the destruction of the suitors.

Laertes is Odysseus' father and a great but aging warrior. He is so distressed by his son's absence that he lives alone and ceases to come into the city. He is happily reunited with Odysseus at the end of the poem.

Anticlea is Odysseus' mother. She dies of grief while Odysseus is away from Ithaca. He meets her as a shade in the underworld but cannot embrace her ghostly form.

Eumaeus is a humble and good-hearted swineherd intensely loyal to the memory of Odysseus. He is gracious and kind to Odysseus when the latter first returns to Ithaca in the guise of a beggar. He assists Odysseus in taking revenge against the suitors and is rewarded with lands and a title.

Eurycleia is Odysseus' childhood nurse and one of the few servants who remain loyal to the memory of Odysseus. While washing his feet when he is still disguised as a beggar, she recognizes a familiar scar on his leg. She drops his feet into the basin and nearly cries out, but Odysseus quiets her and swears her to secrecy. She supports his efforts to oust the suitors.

Philoetius is a goatherd—the only other servant who remains loyal to Odysseus. He is assigned to close the doors of the courtyard during Odysseus' destruction of the suitors.

Menelaus is a great warrior and former fighting companion of Odysseus during the Trojan War. He and his wife, Helen of Troy, offer generous hospitality to Telemachus, telling him stories of his father's exploits during the war. By capturing and questioning Proteus, the old man of the sea, Menelaus discovers that Odysseus is still alive but stranded on the island of Calypso.

Nestor is an old and wise fighting companion of Odysseus. Telemachus visits him on Argos in the hope of finding news of his father.

Calypso is a goddess who falls in love with Odysseus and will not let him leave her island for seven years.

Circe is a goddess whose potion transforms the heads and necks of Odysseus' men into those of pigs. By threatening her and then sleeping with her, Odysseus compels her to change his men back to human form. She takes care of Odysseus and his men for a year before giving them advice about how to make it back to Ithaca and allowing them to depart.

Alcinoos is the king of the Phaeacians. He governs a splendid and well-ordered kingdom. He shows Odysseus great hospitality, entertaining him, giving him gifts, and listening to the great story of his wanderings. He also provides ships and men for Odysseus' long-awaited homecoming to Ithaca.

Arete is the virtuous wife of Alcinoos (her name means "virtue" in Greek). She is queen of Phaeacia.

Nausicaa is the beautiful daughter of Alcinoos and Arete. She discovers Odysseus when he comes ashore on Phaeacia after many days and nights at sea. She is impressed by his appearance and gives him valuable advice about how to gain access to the king and queen.

Demodocos is a blind singer who performs the story of the Trojan Horse for Odysseus and the Phaiakian court. He is often taken to be a figure for Homer himself.

Polyphemus is the brutal one-eyed monster (of the race of beings called Cyclopes) who traps Odysseus and his men in his cave. He dashes out their brains and eats four of them before Odysseus gouges his eye out with a sharpened stick. Odysseus then tricks him several times in effecting an escape. He calls upon his father, Poseidon, to take revenge upon Odysseus.

Eurylachus is Odysseus' second-in-command. He quarrels with Odysseus on several occasions. It is he and his men who are turned into pigs by Circe. It is also he who persuades the men to kill and eat the cattle of Helios, thereby bringing upon himself and his men the deadly vengeance of Zeus.

Elpenor is one of Odysseus' men. On the day that Odysseus and his men leave the house of Circe, he gets drunk and falls asleep on the roof. He later rolls off the roof, breaks his neck, and dies. He meets Odysseus in the underworld and asks for a proper burial, which Odysseus promises and later carries out.

Teiresias is the great prophet with whom Odysseus speaks in the land of the dead. He gives Odysseus precise instructions for returning to Ithaca.

Antinoos and Eurymachus are the haughty and disrespectful leaders of the suitors. They are the first to die when Odysseus returns.

Athena is the goddess of wisdom. She is Odysseus' chief ally among the gods. She appears at many crucial points of the poem to advise and assist Odysseus and Telemachus.

Poseidon is the god of the sea. A great and powerful god, he conceives a grudge against Odysseus when the hero puts out the eye of his son, Polyphemus. He continually frustrates Odysseus' efforts to return to Ithaca, and he plays a part in destroying many of Odysseus' men. Only Athena's intervention with Zeus prevents him from destroying Odysseus as well. ❖

Critical Views

[Aristotle (384–322 B.C.E.) was one of the greatest philosophers of classical antiquity and an enormous influence upon Western thought in the Middle Ages and Renaissance. The *Poetics*—one of several of his treatises devoted to literature and rhetoric—survives only in a fragment; the section we have deals largely with the theory and practice of tragic drama. In this extract, Aristotle praises Homer for achieving unity of form in the *Odyssey* by not telling all the known stories about Odysseus but only those that result in a unified scenario.]

Unity of plot does not, as some persons think, consist in the unity of the hero. For infinitely various are the incidents in one man's life which cannot be reduced to unity; and so, there are many actions of one man out of which we cannot make an action. Hence the error, it appears, of all poets who have composed a *Heracleid,* a *Theseid,* or other poems of the kind. They imagine that as Heracles was one man, the story of Heracles must also be a unity. But Homer, as in all else he is of surpassing merit, here too—whether from art or natural genius—seems to have happily discerned the truth. In composing the *Odyssey* he did not include all the adventures of Odysseus—such as his wound on Parnassus, or his feigned madness at the mustering of the host—incidents between which there was no necessary or probable connexion: but he made the *Odyssey,* and likewise the *Iliad,* to centre round an action that in our sense of the word is one.

> —Aristotle, *Poetics* (c. 335 B.C.E.) 1451a, tr. S. H. Butcher (London: Macmillan, 1895; 4th ed. 1907), pp. 33, 35

LONGINUS ON THE *ODYSSEY* AS THE PRODUCT OF HOMER'S OLD AGE

[Longinus is the name under which the treatise *Peri Hypsous* ("On the Sublime"), written sometime in the first century A.D., has come down to us. Nothing is known about the author, but the work is an important contribution to ancient literary criticism in its keen analysis of style, rhetoric, and literary greatness. In this extract, Longinus claims to deduce from internal evidence that the *Odyssey* is later than the *Iliad* and that it is also the work of Homer's old age.]

It is clear from many indications that the *Odyssey* was his second subject. A special proof is the fact that he introduces in that poem remnants of the adventures before Ilium as episodes, so to say, of the Trojan War. And indeed, he there renders a tribute of mourning and lamentation to his heroes as though he were carrying out a long-cherished purpose. In fact, the *Odyssey* is simply an epilogue to the *Iliad:*—

> There lieth Ajax the warrior wight, Achilles is there,
> There is Patroclus, whose words had weight as a God he were;
> There lieth mine own dear son.

It is for the same reason, I suppose, that he has made the whole structure of the *Iliad,* which was written at the height of his inspiration, full of action and conflict, while the *Odyssey* for the most part consists of narrative, as is characteristic of old age. Accordingly, in the *Odyssey* Homer may be likened to a sinking sun, whose grandeur remains without its intensity. He does not in the *Odyssey* maintain so high a pitch as in those poems of Ilium. His sublimities are not evenly sustained and free from the liability to sink; there is not the same profusion of accumulated passions, nor the supple and oratorical style, packed with images drawn from real life. You seem to see henceforth the ebb and flow of greatness, and a fancy roving in the fabulous and incredible, as though the ocean were withdrawing into itself and were being laid bare within its own confines. In saying this I have not forgotten the tempests in the

Odyssey and the story of the Cyclops and the like. If I speak of old age, it is nevertheless the old age of Homer. The fabulous element, however, prevails throughout this poem over the real. The object of this digression has been, as I said, to show how easily great natures in their decline are sometimes diverted into absurdity, as in the incident of the wine-skin and of the men who were fed like swine by Circe (*whining porkers,* as Zoilus called them), and of Zeus like a nestling nurtured by the doves, and of the hero who was without food for ten days upon the wreck, and of the incredible tale of the slaying of the suitors. For what else can we term these things than veritable dreams of Zeus? These observations with regard to the *Odyssey* should be made for another reason—in order that you may know that the genius of great poets and prose-writers, as their passion declines, finds its final expression in the delineation of character. For such are the details which Homer gives, with an eye to characterisation, of life in the home of Odysseus; they form as it were a comedy of manners.

—Longinus, *On the Sublime* (c. 1st century A.D.), tr. W. Rhys Roberts (Cambridge: Cambridge University Press, 1899), pp. 67, 69

Andrew Lang on Homer's Philosophy of Life

[Andrew Lang (1844–1912) was a prolific Scottish novelist, poet, and critic. He is today perhaps best known for a series of fairy tale collections in which each volume is named after a color, such as *The Blue Fairy Book* (1889). He also wrote a number of whimsical critical essays, including *Letters to Dead Authors* (1886) and *Adventures among Books* (1901). In this extract from his book on *Homer and the Epic* (1893), Lang derives Homer's philosophy of life from his works, maintaining that it is on the whole melancholy but counterbalanced by his belief that life is full of wonders and adventures.]

The philosophy of Homer, simply as his problems are stated, is fortified against all vicissitude. His mind, like the mind of

Herodotus is constantly occupied by the thought of change, how the ancient city must fall, and fall, too, must its conqueror, slain on his own hearthstone in the full fruition of victory. Nay, the very civilisation of which Homer sings, with all its valour and art and gold, is to go down before the assaults of the Dorians. His Achilles is the type of triumphant youth, but of youth with sheer doom before its eyes. To him

> One crowded hour of glorious life
> Is worth an age without a name.

His eyes are open from the first, and his choice is made. This, then, is the philosophy of Homer, and to what other better philosophy have the schools of three thousand years brought their disciples? It is for this clear vision, this lucid insight into the ultimate questions, that Greece chose Homer for the master of masters, the teacher of all philosophers, 'the first of those who know.'

His theory of life might thus be called melancholy. Even at home, after all his wanderings, the curse of the sea god yet hangs over Odysseus, his troubles are not over, he must set forth again into the unheard of lands. There is no continuance of mortal happiness, 'here we have no abiding city,' but against this Homer does not repine. With his clear vision of the end of all living, he combines the gladdest enjoyment of life. To him the world is full of joy. Storms, and snow, and sea, the ruinous rains, the noisy torrents that divide the hills, the eyes of lions, the peaceful piping of the shepherd, the murmur of man and maid from rock and oak-tree, the woven dance, the tribunal, all the arts of ship-building, of gold work, of weaving and embroidery, all the life of peace, of the chase and the festival and the song, all the life of war, ambush, and siege, and march, clashing of shields, and countering of chariots, all is alike dear to him, all makes part of the eternally moving, the eternally absorbing spectacle. His work-a-day world is on every hand environed with the divine, as the refluent stream of Oceanus girdles the earth. The gods appear in beautiful shapes of young men and huntress maidens; in the unsailed seas, the untrodden isles, the goddess burns her fragrant fire, and sings her magic song, as she weaves at the immortal loom. Everything is full of possibilities, every adventure tempts him, whether here he meets the courteous and clement Egyptians, by the river Ægyptus, or there the cannibal Læstrygonians, by their fiord in the land of the midnight sun. This world that is so hard, this life that must end in death, are yet rich in the beautiful and the strange. Man's days are wealthy in works and deeds, he is a warrior, a counsellor, a hunter, a shipwright, a smith, a mower in the fields of hay, a ploughman behind the steers.

This is life, as Homer paints it, life cheered by women as fair as the heroes are bold, ladies loyal, staunch, wise, tender and true, fit mates for the heroes. When the men are dead in battle and eaten of dogs, before the women lies the day of captivity, 'to strew another's bed and bring water from another's well,' but the hour is their own.

Thus Homer takes all experience for his province, in his similes he gives us idylls, 'little pictures' of pastoral or hunting days, encounters with lions, adventures in the mountain mists, wars with the sea waves for home and for dear life, labour in every kind, sketches of children, building houses of sea sand, or clinging to their mother's gown, and crying to be taken up in her arms. He has humour, too, as in his pictures of the squabbles of Olympus, the speeches of Thersites, the arrogance of the wooers, the girl in thought about her wedding day, the easy luxurious Phæacians. 'His lyre has all the chords'—now the triumphant Achæans, bearing Hector dead break into a pæan, now the women shrill the dirge, as even yet they do in Corsica. The epic is thus the sum of all poetry—tragedy, comedy, lyric, dirge, idyll, are all blended in its great furnace into one glorious metal, and one colossal group. Another style of composition Homer offers us, which nowhere else we receive from Greece, till we get it, in decadent though still beautiful shape, in Greece's dying age. The epic, in the *Odyssey,* becomes a romance, the best of all romances, and the most skilfully narrated. No later tale can match, in sheer skill of composition, with the *Odyssey.*

—Andrew Lang, *Homer and the Epic* (London: Longmans, Green, 1893), pp. 4–7

[Samuel Butler (1835–1902), a celebrated English novelist and author of *Erewhon* (1872) and *The Way of All
Flesh* (1902), wrote a whimsical treatise claiming from
internal evidence that the *Odyssey* must have been
written by a woman. He bases this claim on the belief
that the epic is told from the viewpoint of a woman
and that it contains details that only a woman would
know.]

As for the *Odyssey* having been written by a woman, they will
tell me that I have not even established a *primâ facie* case for
my opinion. Of course I have not. It was ⟨Richard⟩ Bentley who
did this, when he said that the *Iliad* was written for men, and
the *Odyssey* for women. The history of literature furnishes us
with no case in which a man has written a great masterpiece
for women rather than men. If an anonymous book strikes so
able a critic as having been written for women, a *primâ facie*
case is established for thinking that it was probably written by a
woman. I deny, however, that the *Odyssey* was written for
women; it was written for any one who would listen to it. What
Bentley meant was that in the *Odyssey* things were looked at
from a woman's point of view rather than a man's, and in utter-
ing this obvious truth, I repeat, he established once for all a
strong *primâ facie* case for thinking that it was written by a
woman. ⟨. . .⟩

It may be urged that it is extremely improbable that any
woman in any age should write such a masterpiece as the
Odyssey. But so it also is that any man should do so. In all the
many hundreds of years since the *Odyssey* was written, no
man has been able to write another that will compare with it. It
was extremely improbable that the son of a Stratford wool-
stapler should write *Hamlet,* or that a Bedfordshire tinker
should produce such a masterpiece as *Pilgrim's Progress.*
Phenomenal works imply a phenomenal workman, but there
are phenomenal women as well as phenomenal men, and
though there is much in the *Iliad* which no woman, however
phenomenal, can be supposed at all likely to have written,
there is not a line in the *Odyssey* which a woman might not
perfectly well write, and there is much beauty which a man

would be almost certain to neglect. Moreover there are many mistakes in the *Odyssey* which a young woman might easily make, but which a man could hardly fall into—for example, making the wind whistle over the waves at the end of Book ii., thinking that a lamb could live on two pulls a day at a ewe that was already milked (ix. 244, 245, and 308, 309), believing a ship to have a rudder at both ends (ix. 483, 540), thinking that dry and well-seasoned timber can be cut from a growing tree (v. 240), making a hawk while still on the wing tear its prey—a thing that no hawk can do (xv. 527). ⟨. . .⟩

So with Calypso's axe (v. 234–36). No one who was used to handling an axe would describe it so fully and tell us that it "suited Ulysses' hands," and was furnished with a handle. I have heard say that a celebrated female authoress was discovered to be a woman by her having spoken of a two-foot *ruler* instead of a two-foot *rule,* but over-minuteness of description is deeper and stronger evidence of unfamiliarity than mistaken nomenclature is.

Such mistakes and self-betrayals as those above pointed out enhance rather than impair the charm of the *Odyssey.* Granted that the *Odyssey* is inferior to the *Iliad* in strength, robustness, and wealth of poetic imagery, I cannot think that it is inferior in its power of fascinating the reader. Indeed, if I had to sacrifice one or the other, I can hardly doubt that I should let the *Iliad* go rather than the *Odyssey*—just as if I had to sacrifice either Mont Blanc or Monte Rosa, I should sacrifice Mont Blanc, though I know it to be in many respects the grander mountain of the two.

—Samuel Butler, *The Authoress of the* Odyssey (1897; rpt. London: Jonathan Cape; New York: E. P. Dutton, 1925), pp. 3–4, 9–10

JOHN A. SCOTT ON ODYSSEUS IN THE *ILIAD* AND THE *ODYSSEY*

[John A. Scott (1867–1947) was an American student of religion and classical antiquity who wrote *The Unity of Homer* (1921), *Socrates and Christ* (1928) and *Homer and His Influence* (1925), from which this extract is taken. Here, Scott compares the role of Odysseus in Homer's two epics, noting both the differences and the similarities in his portrayal.]

Odysseus in the *Iliad* was one of the eight or ten outstanding leaders, but he was clearly not in training for the great part he was to take in the companion poem. When Hector challenged the best of the Greeks to meet him in single combat they decided to select his antagonist by lot, and as the lot was cast they all prayed that "Ajax, Agamemnon, or Diomede might be chosen," but no one wanted Odysseus to have this dangerous honor. In the contest for the prize in archery he did not compete, yet in the *Odyssey* he boasted that he easily excelled all those at Troy who handled the bow.

The hero of the *Odyssey* is a re-creation of the Odysseus of the *Iliad,* the same in gifts, but greatly exalted. Then, too, the wife, Penelope, is never named in the earlier epic. The poet did not introduce the hero in person until in the fifth book of the *Odyssey,* since the impression must be created that he is of such importance that his fate is eagerly discussed not only in Ithaca, Pylos, and Sparta, but among the assembled gods of Olympus as well.

The action of the *Iliad,* as far as the human actors are concerned, is confined to the limited area of the Troad, while the hero of the *Odyssey* moves from Troy to the land of the Cicones, then throughout the length of the Aegean, thence out into fairyland and back to Ithaca. Telemachus journeyed to Pylos and to Sparta, Nestor told of his return voyage from Troy, while Menelaus recounted his adventures in Egypt and his visit to many lands, even to Phoenicia and Libya.

The greatest single difference between the *Iliad* and the *Odyssey* is the difference of setting, for the action of the *Iliad* is confined to a single small district, the action of the *Odyssey* moves without restraint over limitless regions, going even into fairyland and to Hades.

The plot of the *Iliad* is loosely joined, so loosely that there are many books which contribute little or nothing towards the advancement of the story. The sixth, ninth, and twenty-third books are three of the greatest of the poem, yet had they been lost from the manuscripts and never been quoted, one could hardly have suspected their existence. This does not mean that they were additions by later poets, since if most of the soliloquies of *Hamlet* had been lost it would have been hard to detect the gaps. The important eleventh book is only vaguely connected with the books immediately preceding.

In the *Odyssey* the structure is just the reverse, for in it there is such a mutual interchange of cause and effect that each book can be understood only in the light of earlier books. Athena in the first book came from Olympus to arouse Telemachus to go in search of his father; in the second an assembly is called and this search is announced as well as prepared. In this the poet had a double purpose, he showed us the wife, the son, the suitors, the faithful Euryclia, and the conditions in Ithaca, and we are made to realize the great importance of the hero himself.

In the next two books the young man made the trip to Pylos and to Sparta as ordered and planned, and we learn the heroic stature of Odysseus from his own companions and associates at Troy.

Just such an introduction as is given in these books is needed to make the hearer feel that the Odysseus he had known in the *Iliad* is fitted for the great part he was destined to assume. Had the *Odyssey* opened at book five the poet could not have created the impression that the Odysseus he had left at the games of the *Iliad* had become sufficiently important to warrant his holding the center of the stage, and holding it throughout the entire poem. This journey of Telemachus had another purpose and that was the furnishing of an opportunity for the immature youth to develop under new influences into the hero he proved to be in the great struggle with the suitors.

The long story of Odysseus' wanderings could have found no ready and eager audience without the songs of Demodocus and the exploits at the games. Even the mysterious movements through fairyland have a necessary sequence, since the crews who manned the twelve ships with which he sailed from

Troy were far too numerous to be entertained by Circe, hence the destruction of the eleven ships at the hands of the Laestry-gones must precede the story of the sojourn in the Aeaean isle. Even one shipload was too many men for the seven years with Calypso, hence the slaughter of the cattle of the sun and the shipwreck, but the adventures with Charybdis and Scylla demanded a ship and its crew, hence they came earlier than the storm which brought the loss of all his companions.

It is doubtful if the skill with which the poet of the *Odyssey* weaves the individual strands of poetry into a great epic plot has ever been equalled. This is the second great difference between the two poems, since the *Iliad* is a succession of loosely joined scenes, a series of pearls strung on the thread of the anger of Achilles, and so strung that many of them might have been removed without detection, while the *Odyssey* is a complicated chain of poetry, a cable in which each strand strengthens and is strengthened by all the rest.

—John A. Scott, *Homer and His Influence* (Boston: Marshall Jones Co., 1925), pp. 54–58

T. E. SHAW ON HOMER'S TEMPERAMENT

[T. E. Shaw was the pseudonym of T. E. Lawrence (1888–1935), the Welsh intelligence officer who wrote *The Seven Pillars of Wisdom* (1926), an account of his adventures in the Middle East that caused him to be nicknamed "Lawrence of Arabia." Late in life he trans-lated the *Odyssey* into prose, and in his preface he indulges in a somewhat fanciful analysis of Homer's temperament as derived from the *Odyssey*.]

In four years of living with this novel I have tried to deduce the author from his self-betrayal in the work. I found a bookworm, no longer young, living from home, a mainlander, city-bred and domestic. Married but not exclusively, a dog-lover, often hungry and thirsty, dark-haired. Fond of poetry, a great if

41

uncritical reader of the *Iliad*, with limited sensuous range but an exact eyesight which gave him all his pictures. A lover of old bric-a-brac, though as muddled an antiquary as Walter Scott—in sympathy with which side of him I have conceded 'tenter-hooks' but not railway-trains.

It is fun to compare his infuriating male condescension towards inglorious woman with his tender charity of head and heart for serving-men. Though a stickler for the prides of poets and a man who never misses a chance to cocker up their standing, yet he must be (like writers two thousand years after him) the associate of menials, making himself their friend and defender by understanding. Was it a fellow-feeling, or did he forestall time in his view of slavery?

He loved the rural scene as only a citizen can. No farmer, he had learned the points of a good olive tree. He is all adrift when it comes to fighting, and had not seen deaths in battle. He had sailed upon and watched the sea with a palpitant concern, seafaring being not his trade. As a minor sportsman he had seen wild boars at bay and heard tall yarns of lions.

Few men can be sailors, soldiers and naturalists. Yet this Homer was neither land-lubber nor stay-at-home nor ninny. He wrote for audiences to whom adventures were daily life and the sea their universal neighbour. So he dared not err. That famous doubled line where the Cyclops narrowly misses the ship with his stones only shows how much better a seaman he was than his copyist. Scholiasts have tried to riddle his technical knowledge—and of course he does make a hotch-potch of periods. It is the penalty of being prearchaeological. His pages are steeped in a queer naïvety; and at our remove of thought and language we cannot guess if he is smiling or not. Yet there is a dignity which compels respect and baffles us, he being neither simple in education nor primitive socially. His generation so rudely admired the *Iliad* that even to misquote it was a virtue. He sprinkles tags of epic across his pages. In this some find humour. Rather I judge that here too the tight lips of archaic art have grown the fixed grin of archaism.

Very bookish, this house-bred man. His work smells of the literary coterie, of a writing tradition. His notebooks were stocked with purple passages and he embedded these in his tale wherever they would more or less fit. He, like William Morris, was driven by his age to legend, where he found men living untrammelled under the God-possessed skies. Only, with more verbal felicity than Morris', he had less poetry. Fashion gave him recurring epithets, like labels: but repetitions tell, in public speaking. For recitation, too, are the swarming speeches. A trained voice can put drama and incident into speeches. Perhaps the tedious delay of the climax through ten books may be a poor bard's means of prolonging his host's hospitality.

Obviously the tale was the thing; and that explains (without excusing it to our ingrown minds) his thin and accidental characterisation. He thumb-nailed well; and afterwards lost heart. Nausicaa, for instance, enters dramatically and shapes, for a few lines, like a woman—then she fades, unused. Eumaeus fared better: but only the central family stands out, consistently and pitilessly drawn—the sly cattish wife, that cold-blooded egotist Odysseus, and the priggish son who yet met his master-prig in Menelaus. It is sorrowful to believe that these were really Homer's heroes and exemplars.

—T. E. Shaw (T. E. Lawrence), "Translator's Note," *The Odyssey of Homer,* tr. T. E. Shaw (New York: Oxford University Press, 1932), pp. vi–vii

❖

M. I. Finley on the Religion of Homer

[M. I. Finley (1912–1986) was one of the most distinguished classical scholars of his generation. He was Emeritus Fellow of Darwin College, Cambridge, and wrote many books, including *Aspects of Antiquity* (1968; rev. 1977), *Early Greece* (1970; rev. 1981), and *Ancient Slavery and Modern Ideology* (1980). In this extract from his book on Homer, Finley studies the gods in the *Iliad* and the *Odyssey,* claiming that they differ fundamentally from our conception of godhead by being essentially devoid of ethical qualities but also failing to inspire awe and fear.]

In a famous passage in his autobiography, John Stuart Mill wrote of his father: "I have a hundred times heard him say that all ages and nations have represented their gods as wicked, in a constantly increasing progression; that mankind have gone on adding trait after trait till they reached the most perfect conception of wickedness which the human mind can devise, and have called this God, and prostrated themselves before it." For Homeric religion, at least, this is not a pertinent judgment, not because Homer's gods were not wicked, but because they were essentially devoid of any ethical quality whatsoever. The ethics of the world of Odysseus were man-made and man-sanctioned. Man turned to the gods for help in his manifold activities, for the gifts it was in their power to offer or to withhold. He could not turn to them for moral guidance; that was not in their power.

When Odysseus awoke on Ithaca, Athena appeared to him in the guise of a shepherd and was greeted by one of Odysseus' characteristic inventions, how he came from Crete, fought at Troy, slew the son of Idomeneus, fled to the Phoenicians, and so forth. Athena smiled, resumed her female shape, and offered the following comment: "Crafty must he be and shifty who would outstrip you in all kinds of cunning, even though it be a god that encountered you. Headstrong man, full of wiles, of cunning insatiate, are you not to cease, even in your own land, from deceit and artful tales, so dear to you from the bottom of your heart? But come, let us speak no more of these things, being both practiced in craft; for you are far the best of all mortals in counsel and speech, and I am celebrated among all the gods in craft and cunning."

This is what the long line of philosophers from Xenophanes to Plato protested, the indifference of the Homeric gods in moral matters. Just before the close of the *Iliad*, Achilles stated the doctrine explicitly: "For two jars stand on Zeus's threshold whence he gives of his evil gifts, and another of the good; and to whom Zeus who delights in thunder gives a mixed portion, to him befalls now evil, now good; but to whom he gives of the baneful, him he scorns, and evil misery chases him over the noble earth, a wanderer honored neither by gods nor by mortals."

Chance, not merit, determined how the gifts fell to a man. And since it was not in his power to influence the choice, man could neither sin nor atone. He could offend a god mightily, but only by dishonoring him, by shaming him—through a false oath, for example, or disobedience of the direct command of an oracle or failure to make a sacrificial gift—and then it was incumbent upon the offender to make amends precisely as he made amends to any man he might have dishonored. But this was not penance; it was the re-establishment of the proper status relationship. Without sin there could be no idea of conscience, no feelings of moral guilt. The evils of which Achilles spoke were mishaps, not the evils of the Decalogue.

And there was no reverential fear of the gods. "Homer's princes bestride their world boldly; they fear the gods only as they fear their human overlords." No word for "god-fearing" is ever used in the *Iliad*. Nor, it scarcely need be added, was there a word for "love of God": *philotheos* makes its first appearance in the language with Aristotle. For moral support the men of the *Iliad* relied not on the gods but on their fellow men, on the institutions and the customs by which they lived; so complete was the intellectual revolution that had occurred. Having lifted the incubus of unintelligible and all-powerful natural forces, man retained a consciousness that there were powers in the universe which he could not control and could not really understand, but he introduced a great self-consciousness, a pride and a confidence in himself, in man and his ways in society.

—M. I. Finley, *The World of Odysseus* (New York: Viking Press, 1954), pp. 149–51

George de F. Lord on the Phaeacian Episode

[George de F. Lord (b. 1919), a former professor of English at Yale University, has written many books of literary criticism, including *Homeric Renaissance: The*

Odyssey *of George Chapman* (1956), *Heroic Mockery* (1977), and *Trials of the Self* (1983). In this extract, Lord studies the Phaeacian episode and believes it to be critical in the shift of focus in the *Odyssey* from fantastic adventure to domestic values.]

The chief importance of the Phaeacian experience lies in its dramatizing a new attitude in Odysseus. His emergence from the supernatural world of Lotus Eaters, Cyclopes, Circe, and Calypso has involved, as I have shown, a recognition of the conditions of being human: mortality, limited power and wisdom, and the need for divine assistance. Odysseus' ready acceptance by Alcinous, Arete, and Nausicaa depends on his acceptance of their own social, religious, and political ideal. Phaeacia has all the earmarks of an ideal civilization with just enough defects to make the whole picture plausible. The Phaeacians are conspicuously peace-loving. They do not use warfare and migrated long ago from a land beset by the godless Cyclopes to this remote place. The gods, they say, are in the habit of visiting them without disguise. They are charitable to strangers. They excel in the arts of peace—in shipbuilding, sailing, spinning and weaving, and so forth. The queen Arete is the real ruler of the kingdom and settles the disputes of her subjects to the invariable satisfaction of both parties. Odysseus kneels to her for permission to sail for Ithaca and by this action pays tribute to the domestic ideals which Arete stands for. Arete is, perhaps, almost impossibly wise and competent, but Nausicaa stands in the foreground as an extraordinarily real young girl. As Mr. Post says, "It is here that the climax of temptation comes for Odysseus. It is characteristic of Homer to make his good woman more tempting than any bad woman could be."

For Odysseus Nausicaa serves as an enchanting vision of the new ideal, just as fading Helen, with her ornamental distaff and her anodynes, provided Telemachus with a *fin de siècle* vision of the heroic past. Nausicaa appeals to Odysseus by virtue of qualities which make his surrender to her impossible: by her hospitality and charity and courage and deep loyalty to the civilized institutions to which he is now dedicated. In her consuming interest in marriage and in family and household affairs he may well see an image of his own wife. Thus he treats her with unwonted tact and restraint. His manner is a judicious mixture of the gallant and the paternal. With the immortal Circe and Calypso Odysseus had no age, but with Nausicaa he is a mature man. Much of the humor in their encounter stems from this discrepancy of ages which attracts them to each other and yet helps to keep them apart. His famous words on their first meeting, when he emerges so delightfully from the underbrush naked and holding an olive-branch modestly before him, set the tone of the whole episode:

> Show me the city and give me some rag to throw about me. . . . For thyself, may the gods grant thee all thy heart desires—a husband and a home and oneness of heart—great gifts. For nothing is finer than when husband and wife live in one house in one accord, a great grief to their foes and a joy to their friends. But they themselves know this best. (VI, 178–85)

This note is struck again in that exquisite farewell interlude in which Odysseus gently deflects Nausicaa's growing love for him by pretending not to understand her Desdemona-like hints:

> Now when the maids had bathed him and rubbed him with oil and had cast a fine cloak and tunic about him, he came from the bath and went to join the men at their wine. Nausicaa, gifted with beauty by the gods, stood by the doorpost of the hall and watched Odysseus with wonder and spoke to him with winged words:
> "Farewell, stranger, and hereafter even in thine own native land remember me, for to me thou owest thy life."
> Then the wily Odysseus answered her:
> "Nausicaa, daughter of great-hearted Alcinous, may Zeus, the loud-thundering lord of Hera grant that I reach my home and see the day of my return. Then I will pray to thee as a god all my days, for thou, maiden, hast given me life." (VIII, 454–68)

If Odysseus' rejection of Calypso's offer of immortality was a rejection of a sort of eternal and monotonous existence approximating death, the endless cycle of instinctive gratifications which left the spirit unsatisfied, his rejection of Nausicaa represents, paradoxically enough, his acceptance of a way of life which is more than mere existence. He now sees his own identity bound up with Penelope's. Away from home he is not himself.

I do not think it is doing violence to this crucial phase of the *Odyssey* to see in the Phaeacian visit a sort of spiritual and ideological revolution in the hero. This involves his reorientation in regard to the dominant values of the poem—the domestic and social values of which I have been speaking. Nor do I think it extravagant to insist that these values which center on the family, on the pre-eminent virtue of hospitality, and on the just administration of the state are shown throughout the poem as superior to what might be loosely designated as the heroic values of the *Iliad*. (In saying this I do not mean to imply that Homer gives unqualified assent to these values in the *Iliad*.) What threatens these domestic values is the old ideal of military glory and honor as man's noblest goal—the individualistic quest for eternal fame in battle. The *Odyssey* never disdains true honor as such, and in the slaughter of the suitors it recognizes that the most extreme punitive measures may sometimes be needed to protect society, but it submits what passes for honor to a searching inspection and shows that heroic deeds are often motivated by greed, accomplished with terror, and indistinguishable from piracy. In this poem Odysseus' career evolves from one set of values toward the other, from the narrow concepts of heroic honor to the broader concepts of the civilized man in a post-war world. Odysseus is not given to introspection, and his change of view is presented in a series of episodes that are emblematic of inner developments. Of these there are three main kinds: (1) a divine visitation; (2) an unexpected emotional response; and (3) a speech in which the hero analyzes his experiences in a way that lets us see implications of which he is only partly aware.

—George de F. Lord, "The *Odyssey* and the Western World," *Sewanee Review* 62, No. 3 (July–September 1954): 417–20

W. B. STANFORD ON ODYSSEUS AS A FIGURE OF FOLKLORE

[W. B. Stanford (1910–1984) is the author of *Ambiguity in Greek Literature* (1939), *The Quest for Ulysses*

(1974; with J. V. Luce), and an edition and commentary of the *Odyssey* (1947–48). In this extract from his book, *The Ulysses Theme* (1954), a study of the influence of the *Odyssey* upon subsequent literature, Stanford shows that Homer probably did not invent Odysseus but that he adapted a folklore figure around whom a number of stories and legends had already clustered.]

As far as extant literature goes the story of Ulysses begins in the *Iliad* and the *Odyssey*. Earlier records have not revealed any definite references to it, as yet. But Ulysses was apparently not Homer's own invention, and Homer never suggests it. On the contrary he makes it clear by implication that Ulysses was already a familiar figure when he began to write about him. Ulysses appears in both poems without any preliminary introductions; incidents in his career which lie outside the main story of the *Iliad* and *Odyssey* are alluded to casually, as if on the understanding that everyone knew their main features; and Ulysses's stock epithets imply that at least some of his characteristics were proverbial before Homer adopted him as his chief hero.

This is not conclusive evidence. One cannot be quite certain when a sophisticated writer like Homer endows one of his characters with a traditional background that this is not simply a device for enhancing the prestige of a newcomer. There are, however, other indications that Ulysses was not Homer's own invention. First, there is the extraordinary variation in the spelling of his name. In Greek alone there are twelve variations ranging from *Odysseus* to *Oulixes*. No other mythological name shows anything like the same variety. If these mutations are to be explained in terms of normal linguistic processes, the main variants must have emerged long before Homer's time. On the other hand there may originally have been two separate figures, one called something like *Odysseus,* the other something like *Ulixes,* who were combined into one complex personality. But this still implies the existence of a Ulysses-figure before Homer, for it is unlikely that post-Homeric writers would have introduced the name Ulixes and its cognates to describe a hero invented and originally named Odysseus by Homer.

Purely literary creations like Falstaff, Don Quixote, and Pickwick generally retain, more or less, the names given to them by their creators, no matter how far their legend travels. It seems, then, that whether linguistic mutation or mythological syncretism was the cause of the variations in Ulysses's name, the Ulysses-Odysseus figure was older than Homer.

Secondly, some at least of the motifs in Homer's account of Ulysses seem to have been taken from older sources. To mention only the most remarkable example: over two hundred and twenty versions of the Cyclops incident have been collected from sources extending from India to Ireland. Many of these probably derive directly or indirectly from Homer's narrative. But some seem to incorporate older elements; and some have been found in regions where Homeric influence is improbable. The probability is that this part, at least, of the *Odyssey* goes back to a pre-Homeric source, though it is an open question whether its original hero had any name like Ulysses or Odysseus.

These internal and external indications of earlier origins have prompted many theories on the nature of the pre-Homeric Ulysses. They are mainly historical, religious, or anthropological. Obviously the primeval Ulysses may have been a historical person, a prince of Ithaca endowed with unusual mental ability and renowned for adventurous sea voyages, as Homer asserts; or else an Egyptian trader, or a captain in some Minoan fleet. Or else, as other scholars suggest, he may have been a pre-Greek sea-god (whence the enmity of his Olympian successor, Poseidon), or a solar divinity, or a year-daimon. Anthropologists have dwelt on certain primitive-looking features in his myth, finding traces of a bear or horse fetish, or a Wolf Dietrich, in his description. These far-reaching theories undoubtedly explain some details in Homer's narrative, and it may be that at an early stage in the evolution of the pre-Homeric Ulysses myth elements of this kind were incorporated into it. But since the fully developed personality of Ulysses as portrayed by Homer seems to owe little to remote divine or bestial origins, they will not be studied further here. Historical explanations could, on the other hand, be more helpful in explaining Ulysses's status in Homer. But in fact there is no genuine documentary evidence for the prototypal Ulysses outside Homer.

Until there is, it will remain impossible to determine precisely
what is fact and what fiction in the Homeric poems.

> —W. B. Stanford, *The Ulysses Theme: A Study in the
> Adaptability of a Traditional Hero* (Oxford: Basil Blackwell,
> 1954), pp. 8–9

DENYS PAGE ON THE *ODYSSEY* AS AN ORAL POEM

[Denys Page is an important classical scholar who has
written several controversial books, including *History
and the Homeric* Iliad (1959) and *Folktales in Homer's*
Odyssey (1973). In this extract from his earlier book on
the *Odyssey,* Page builds upon the work of Milman
Parry in studying how Homer's works were initially set
down not by writing but by an oral method involving
systematic repetitions of word-patterns.]

If it is our desire to discover how the *Odyssey* was composed,
to look into the minds and methods of Greek Epic poets in the
centuries before the dawn of history, to understand and evalu-
ate their achievement, it is absolutely necessary first to recognize how great a gulf divides two kinds of poetry—that which
is composed and remembered in the mind, *without* the aid of
writing, and that which is composed *with* the aid of writing.
That the Homeric poems were composed and carried in the
mind, and recited by word of mouth, and that this was the only
method of their composition, and this for a long time the only
mode of their publication to the audiences for which they were
designed—the proof of these things is the outstanding
achievement of an American scholar, Milman Parry, whose pre-
mature death extinguished the brightest light that has been
shed on the Greek Epic in our time.

In societies where the art of writing is unknown, the poet
makes his verses out of metrical formulas—fixed groups of
words, traditional phrases descriptive of particular ideas and
readily adaptable to similar ideas; the stock of such formulas,
gradually accumulated over a long period of time, supplies the

poet at need with a whole group of lines, or a single line, or a part of a line, all ready-made. He cannot stop to meditate while he recites; he cannot read over—let alone change—what he composed a few hundred lines ago; he cannot plan in advance except in very broad outline. But whatever he wants to say, within the limits of certain traditional themes, may (and often must) be expressed in phrases long ago designed for that purpose, and immediately suggested to him by his practised memory. He may or may not be a good poet: he must be a good craftsman. There is a stock-in-trade, the vast number of traditional formulas, to be learnt only by long apprenticeship; and there is a technique, the craft of using and adapting formulas and systems of formulas, to be acquired only by long experience.

The Homeric Epic differs from all other Greek poetry, and from all poetry with which we (most of us) are familiar today, in just this respect: its elements are phrases, not words. It is largely composed of traditional formulas, fixed word-patterns, almost infinitely adaptable to the ideas suggested to the poet's imagination within the limits of his theme; and supplying lines, or parts of lines, more or less ready-made. In the *Iliad* and *Odyssey* this technique may be seen at a very advanced state of development, refined and thrifty, purified of superfluities, so that (in general) one formula cannot take the place of another, in the same part of the verse, without altering the meaning of what is being said. If the poet wishes to begin his verse with the thought 'But when they arrived . . .', he has one way, and one only, of expressing this, *autar epei rh' ikonto*, 'denying himself all other ways of expressing the idea'. The creation of the vast number of formulas, adaptable to almost all possible emergencies, must have been the work of many generations of poets; and from the refinement, thrift, and economy of the Homeric stock of phrases we are obliged to infer that we are at or near the culmination of a very long process.

Now the *Odyssey*, no less than the *Iliad*, is composed in this way: it reveals from start to finish the memory-technique of verse-making, the practice of composing from memory without the aid of writing. Whether the art of writing was known to its composers we may never know: what we do know, because we see it with our own eyes, is that the art of writing, if it was familiar, made little or no difference to the technique employed in the actual verse-making; that is still the formula-technique, the building of verses out of traditional phrases learnt by one generation from another and supplied to the poet by his practised memory at the moment required.

There is no longer any doubt about the fact; but one may well wonder whether it does not suggest some further questions of exceptional difficulty. Is not the complexity of the structure of the *Odyssey*—its blend of three stories into one; its blend of episodes within one story—beyond the limit of what is possible for a man who has nothing but his memory to assist him? And would not a poem thus composed be continually changing? Would it not differ from one recitation to another, and would it not become unrecognizably transformed in the course of a generation or two? Modern analogies confirm what common sense suggests—that 'the oral poem even in the mouth of the same singer is ever in a state of change; and it is the same when his poetry is sung by others'.

These are difficult questions; I do no more than indicate the region in which their answer may be found. It is possible, or even likely, that the art of writing was practised (though not in general use) at the time when the first continuous *Odyssey* was composed. Now though that art played little or no part in the making of the poem, it might nevertheless be used to record the poem when made (or rather while making). If this were so, the boundaries of the poet's powers would be greatly extended: he could then build, as nobody before such a time could build, a structure of considerable size and some complexity, if each development was preserved in writing; and his admirers or apprentices would be able to reproduce their master's voice much more faithfully than before, not because they could learn it from the written record—that was merely the architect's plan, not his structure—but because the version which they heard from the master was more or less unvarying. This does not imply that the master himself (and others after him) would cease to expand or otherwise alter his poem in the course of time: the written record is nothing more than an aid to memory, a tool of the trade. The text of a poem was still the spoken, not the written, word; the whole conception of a static poem in a standard text is entirely foreign to the memory-technique of verse-making and to the manner of its transmission from one generation to another.

—Denys Page, *The Homeric* Odyssey (Oxford: Clarendon Press, 1955), pp. 138–41

❖

CEDRIC H. WHITMAN ON THE DIFFERENCES BETWEEN THE *ILIAD* AND THE *ODYSSEY*

[Cedric H. Whitman (1916–1979) was Eliot Professor of Greek at Harvard University. He wrote *Sophocles: A Study of Heroic Humanism* (1951), *Euripides and the Full Circle of Myth* (1974), *The Heroic Paradox* (1982), and other works. In this extract from his book on Homer, Whitman studies the shift in psychology one finds between the *Iliad* and the *Odyssey,* in that the former seems to focus on death while the latter champions the prodigious variety of life.]

The masterpieces of the Geometric Age were funerary, and their memorial purpose is revealed in the death-like quietude of their formality. They have the heroic death-consciousness which pervades the *Iliad.* The focus of the *Odyssey,* on the other hand, is life in all its variety and directness, and again recalls the more lyrical responses of proto-Attic art, where life as daily lived and observed, unmediated by anything but the senses, finds its first expression since the fall of the Bronze Age, and thereby lays the foundation of the so-called "Greek renaissance." Such a shift reflects a shift in the psychology of a people. Ordinarily it is said that the Greek renaissance was a period of rising individualism and the discovery of the self as such. Yet the *Iliad* is a poem of self-knowledge in every sense as much as the *Odyssey,* but whereas the latter exhibits a hero whose will is proverbial for its unity and tenacity, the *Iliad*'s hero is the first in our history to be divided by the metaphysical paradox of human nature. Achilles allies himself with equal intensity, both to his own human nature, with all its concern and commitments, and to that intuition of the absolute in being and value which is the besetting demon of the spiritual hero. These opposites can be joined only in the mysterious flame of a love at once detached and entire, self-discovery in self-destruction. Achilles stands representative in and of an architectonic world in which everything is known and in its place, except himself; his learning of himself is a creating of himself. Death is always imminently upon him, a formative limitation which reveals itself at last as the inevitable framework of his tragic being. By contrast, the life-consciousness of the *Odyssey* involves a vastly different view of the individual soul. In and of himself, the hero is a fixed personality, confronted by no hopeless division in himself; he is equipped, as if by magic, with every skill which any situation might require, so that he needs only to deliberate ways and means; in the whole course of the poem, his celebrated intellect deals with no problem which can even remotely be called intellectual, and least of all does he deal with that deepest of all intellectual problems, the self. He is himself—at least if viewed from one point of view. Yet from another point of view, the matter is more mysterious. Life's paradox now appears not in the man but in his external experience, and the adventures of Odysseus, both on the sea and in Ithaca, cast upon him a constantly shifting cloud of disguise, from which he never fully emerges until he has revealed himself to the last person to whom he must—Laertes. And it is by no means tactless of the poet to have saved Laertes till last, incidentally, for recognition by one's father is, in a way, the final legitimation which establishes a man in his world. And it is the world which is the overt concern of Odysseus. Achilles created himself; Odysseus creates his world, by risk, choice, tenacity, and action, and the world thus created reveals the selfhood of its creator. By contact with the "limits of the earth," Odysseus defines, rather than discovers, himself, each experience involving, and at last dissipating, a particular shade of that anonymity which overhangs a man until his context is complete. Hence in the first part of the poem Odysseus is regularly an unknown man to those who receive him, until by some word of action he makes his identity known. In the second part, his disguise conceals him, except at such times when the truth peeps out a little, for the astute to read. Mephistopheles promised to show Faust "first the small world, then the great," and through such experience Faust expands beyond the limits of his earlier self to a transcendent knowledge. The *Odyssey* exactly reverses this process. Odysseus begins, equipped with knowledge so various as to be in a sense transcendental, in the great world of magic and mysterious, absolute existences, and slowly by determination narrows it all down to the small circle of his own family household. And by contrast with the *Iliad,* where the world was architectonic and the hero the measure of the infinite, the *Odyssey* presents an infinite and rather amorphous world, under the image of the sea, out of whose mists any monstrosity or beguiling vision may arise, while the hero is the measure of fixity and definition. Perhaps for this reason the *Odyssey* has always seemed the more closely allied, of the two epics, to the classical period, for then too the prevailing outlook centered the legislating mind of the individual as the measure amid unpredictable experience, and infinite possibility. Indeed, it was precisely this view of the individual self, not the *Iliad*'s view, which began to take conscious shape in the seventh century, and to create the new lyrical forms. The *Iliad*'s view returns only in Sophoclean tragedy.

—Cedric H. Whitman, *Homer and the Heroic Tradition* (Cambridge, MA: Harvard University Press, 1958), pp. 295–97

MAURICE BLANCHOT ON THE SIRENS

[Maurice Blanchot (b. 1907) is a leading French literary critic and theorist and the author of many books; among those translated into English are *The Space of Literature* (1982), *The Writing of Disaster* (1986), and *The Infinite Conversation* (1993). In this extract, Blanchot writes in a characteristically prose-poetic manner about the Sirens, probing the many paradoxes in their conception.]

The Sirens: evidently they really sang, but in a way that was not satisfying, that only implied in which direction lay the true sources of the song, the true happiness of the song. Nevertheless, through their imperfect songs which were only a song still to come, they guided the sailor towards that space where singing would really begin. They were therefore not deceiving him; they were really leading him to his goal. But what happened when he reached that place? What was that place? It was a place where the only thing left was to disappear, because in this region of source and origin, music itself had disappeared more completely than in any other place in the world; it was like a sea into which the living would sink with their ears closed and where the Sirens, too, even they, as proof of their good will, would one day have to disappear.

What sort of song was the Sirens' song? What was its defect? Why did this defect make it so powerful? The answer some people have always given is that it was an inhuman song—no doubt a natural noise (what other kind is there?), but one that remained in the margins of nature; in any case, it was foreign to man, and very low, awakening in him that extreme delight in falling which he cannot satisfy in the normal conditions of his life. But, others say, there was something even stranger in the enchantment: it caused the Sirens merely to reproduce the ordinary singing of mankind, and because the Sirens, who were only animals—very beautiful animals because they reflected womanly beauty—could sing the way men sing, their song became so extraordinary that it created in anyone who heard it a suspicion that all human singing was really inhuman. Was it despair, then, that killed men moved to passion by their own singing? That despair verged upon rapture. There was something marvellous about the song: it actually existed, it was ordinary and at the same time secret, a simple, everyday song which they were suddenly forced to recognize, sung in an unreal way by strange powers, powers which were, in a word, imaginary; it was a song from the abyss and once heard it opened an abyss in every utterance and powerfully enticed whoever heard it to disappear into that abyss.

Remember that this song was sung to sailors, men prepared to take risks and fearless in their impulses, and it was a form of navigation too: it was a distance, and what it revealed was the possibility of traveling that distance, of making the song into a movement towards the song and of making this movement into the expression of the greatest desire. Strange navigation, and what was its goal? It has always been possible to believe that those who approached it were not able to do more than approach it, that they died from impatience, from having said too soon: "Here it is; here is where I will drop anchor." Others have claimed that, on the contrary, it was too late: the goal had always been overshot; the enchantment held out an enigmatic promise and through this promise exposed men to the danger of being unfaithful to themselves, unfaithful to their human song and even to the essence of song, by awakening in them hope and the desire for a marvellous beyond, and that beyond was only a desert, as though the region where music originated was the only place completely without music, a sterile dry place where silence, like noise, burned all access to the song in anyone who had once had command of it. Does this mean that there was something evil in the invitation which issued from the depths? Were the Sirens nothing more than unreal voices, as custom would have us believe, unreal voices which were not supposed to be heard, a deception intended to seduce, and which could only be resisted by disloyal or cunning people?

Men have always made a rather ignoble effort to discredit the Sirens by accusing them flatly of lying: they were liars when they sang, frauds when they sighed, fictions when they were touched—nonexistent in every way; and the good sense of Ulysses was enough to do away with this puerile nonexistence.

It is true, Ulysses did overcome them, but how did he do it? Ulysses—the stubbornness and caution of Ulysses, the treachery by which he took pleasure in the spectacle of the Sirens without risking anything and without accepting the consequences; this cowardly, mediocre and tranquil pleasure, this moderate pleasure, appropriate to a Greek of the period of decadence who never deserved to be the hero of the *Iliad;* this happy and confident cowardice, rooted in a privilege which set him apart from the common condition, the others having no right to such elite happiness but only to the pleasure of seeing their leader writhe ludicrously, grimacing with ecstasy in empty space, but also a right to the satisfaction of gaining mastery over their master (no doubt this was the lesson they learned, this was for them the true song of the Sirens): Ulysses' attitude, the amazing deafness of a man who is deaf because he can hear, was enough to fill the Sirens with a despair which until then had been felt only by men, and this despair turned them into real and beautiful girls, just this once real and worthy of their promise, and therefore capable of vanishing into the truth and depth of their song.

Even once the Sirens had been overcome by the power of technology, which will always claim to trifle in safety with un-real (inspired) powers, Ulysses was still not free of them. They enticed him to a place which he did not want to fall into and, hidden in the heart of the *Odyssey,* which had become their tomb, they drew him—and many others—into that happy, unhappy voyage which is the voyage of the tale—of a song which is no longer immediate, but is narrated, and because of this made to seem harmless, an ode which has turned into an episode.

—Maurice Blanchot, "The Song of the Sirens: Encountering the Imaginary" (1959), *The Gaze of Orpheus and Other Literary Essays,* tr. Lydia Davis (Barrytown, NY: Station Hill Press, 1981), pp. 105–7

CHARLES H. TAYLOR, JR. ON CALYPSO AND CIRCE

[Charles H. Taylor, Jr. (b. 1928) is the author of *The Early Collected Editions of Shelley's Poems* (1958) and the editor of *Essays on the* Odyssey (1963). In this extract, Taylor discusses Calypso and Circe as two of the temptations placed in Odysseus' way, showing that they represent different aspects of creative and destructive femininity.]

In many of Odysseus' other adventures, the temptation to sur-render his individual identity is perhaps less obvious, but no less real. Beautiful and soft, Calypso carries the appeal of the eternal feminine. She offers Odysseus much more than the lotus can: not only an escape from physical suffering, but lovely sexuality and eternal life as well. Not only will the environment nurture him like an infant in the womb—note the image of Calypso's cave—but, unlike the infant, he will retain his identity as a male and be able to share the pleasures of sexual differentiation with the goddess. But this is all he will retain of his identity, for with Calypso he can no longer be Odysseus the hero. If he accepts Calypso's offer, he will be no more than the consort of a minor goddess. Impervious to death he will remain, to be sure, but for that very reason he will be unable to run any of the risks which make survival a heroic achievement. Instead, he would have to surrender himself to the instinctual female principle, physically vital, but intellectually and spiritually lifeless. Odysseus' surrender to Calypso would involve the loss both of his outward identity as *polytlas* Odysseus, the man who suffers and endures, and of his inner identity as a separate individual free to come to terms with life on his own. He would have no self, but would exist only as an appendage to the goddess, serving her desire.

Odysseus refuses Calypso's offer of bodily immortality for the same reasons that he resists bodily death: in neither case could be preserve his whole being as Odysseus. Fleshly immortality with Calypso is no more complete than the fleshless immortality so forcefully disparaged by Achilles.

Calypso, Athene tells Zeus at the beginning of the poem, is trying to make Odysseus forget Ithaca; the analogy with the temptation of the Lotus-eaters is clear enough. What is perhaps less clear is that Circe's charms are directed to the same end. She drugs Odysseus' men, not at once to turn them to swine, but *hina panchy lathoiato patridos aies* (10.236), "that they might quite forget their native land." Only after the drug takes effect does she strike them with her rod and pen them in her sties. The sequence of events is significant because it presents the metamorphosis as a corollary of forgetting one's native land. The transformation of man to animal is a vivid image of the lessening of human consciousness which forgetting one's origins implies. Men who let themselves be drugged into a lower level of awareness by the destructive power of the enchantress, the story suggests, become no more than animals to be kept as the woman's pets.

But for Odysseus the consequences of encountering Circe are very different. Homer says that Hermes gave Odysseus the herb moly as an antidote to the enchantress' potion. Yet who has a better claim to divine aid than Odysseus? Possessing more intelligence and willpower than other men, he is ideally equipped to resist the hypnotic powers of Circe's enchantment. She herself never complains that Odysseus has been aided by a god; rather, her response to Odysseus' refusal to succumb to her potion is that he is a man whose mind is proof against enchantment. Unable to subdue him, with characteristic womanly duality she desires to surrender herself instead, imploring him to come to her bed. He, in turn, is obligated to accept her offer, once he is assured he can do so on his own terms. To avoid submission to Circe's destructive power does not mean that her positive feminine values need be rejected. On the contrary, Odysseus' heroic individuality is partly defined by his capacity to encounter the essence of the female principle without being overwhelmed by it.

Circe, then, embodies both the destructive and the creative aspects of the feminine, and Odysseus profits from the latter. It is scarcely surprising that he finds her exotic knowledge and complex sexuality more interesting than Calypso's immortal ease. He enjoys her company so much that even after a year he has to be prodded by his men into continuing on his way.

—Charles H. Taylor, Jr., "The Obstacles to Odysseus' Return,"
Yale Review 50, No. 4 (Summer 1961): 571–73

G. S. KIRK ON THE *ODYSSEY* AS A LESS TRAGIC POEM THAN THE *ILIAD*

[G. S. Kirk (b. 1921), Regius Professor of Greek and Fellow of Trinity College, Cambridge, is an important classical scholar and author of *The Nature of Greek Myths* (1974), *Homer and the Oral Tradition* (1976), and *The* Iliad: *A Commentary* (1985–93). In this extract, Kirk compares the *Iliad* and the *Odyssey* and, like many scholars of classical antiquity, concludes that the *Odyssey* is inferior to the *Iliad* for being less grandly tragic and aristocratic.]

⟨. . .⟩ the *Odyssey* as a whole fails to achieve the profound monumental effect of the *Iliad*. This is partly because the main theme is less universal and less tragic; but to a large extent it is caused by the actual character of Odysseus. The man of many trials and many devices, the canny, suspicious, boastful and ruseful victim of fortune and his own qualities, is obviously less magnificent than the god-like Achilles, the swift and insanely proud warrior; he is also less real, strangely enough, and less credible. Achilles is often petty and unimaginative, in many ways like a destructive and acquisitive child, but there is something sympathetic in him: he represents some of the commonest aspirations and failings of human nature, though on a superhuman scale. Odysseus is a more specialized being, a curious mixture of heroic and intellectual qualities that can never have been frequent in any society. Moreover he is not drawn in much depth: partly the difficulty lies in reconciling the Iliadic Odysseus, who is clever and persuasive but still a great warrior in the classic mould, with the ingenious braggart, poisoned arrows and all, that he has become in some parts of the *Odyssey*. For even within the *Odyssey* itself his character is inconsistent in—for the unitarian audience—a rather unfathomable way. The faithful husband who rejects a life of divinity with Circe and Calypso is estimable enough; he makes a nice symbol of the conservative and social demands of man and the power of his affections, even at the cost of survival; yet he does not accord with the dangerously conceited victor over the Cyclops. In fact this Odysseus of the sea-adventures makes too strong an impression for the good of the whole poem, in the rest of which the hero's character is more consistently sound and gentle—though always suspicious. Admittedly the hero of the false tales is not usually an appealing figure, and one suspects that the real Odysseus quite admired his creations; but otherwise the generous master of servants, the patient victim of insults, the determined and ultimately affectionate husband, is admirable enough. The trouble is that he does not turn out to be very interesting. Largely this is because of the role the main poet has seen fit to assign to Athene, and to the altered conception, different from that of the *Iliad*, of the way in which the gods rule the life of mortals. During the sea-adventures, at least, Athene is absent from Odysseus's side—because she could not risk offending Poseidon, as she explains later, but also perhaps because some of the earlier sea-tales did not have this kind of divine participant; and, though the audience still knows that the hero will survive, his ordeals seem more terrifying as a consequence. Once he is accompanied at almost every step by the goddess, either heavily disguised or in her plainest anthropomorphic form of a tall, beautiful and accomplished woman, the tension of Odysseus's actions and dangers is surely reduced. This may not seriously affect his moral stature, but it diminishes his interest as a hero developing with his circumstances. The growth of Telemachus's character under the goddess's guidance is heavily emphasized; but his father is too mature and too cunning for this kind of unfolding, and the only quirks and anomalies of his character, as we have seen, are probably the rather worrying product of the conflation of different themes and different kinds of epic material. The Achilles of the *Iliad* stands in contrast: he is fascinating because he occasionally rebels against the traditions of the hero. In IX he sublimates his personal affront into a temporary inquietude with the whole concept of heroic warfare and heroic guest-friend obligations, and shows a touch of schizophrenia (or at least hysteria) in the process; while at the poem's end his frenetic mutilation of Hector is followed by a mercurial and heroic acceptance of Zeus's rebuke, and his treatment of Priam reveals a touchy and evanescent humanity that was neither impossible nor entirely expected of him.

—G. S. Kirk, *The Songs of Homer* (Cambridge: Cambridge University Press, 1962), pp. 364–66

C. M. Bowra on the Monsters in the *Odyssey*

[C. M. Bowra (1898–1971) was a Fellow of Wadham College, Oxford, and a prolific critic of ancient and modern literature. Among his books are *Tradition and Design in the* Iliad (1930), *The Greek Experience* (1957), and *Periclean Athens* (1971). In this extract,

Bowra examines the various monsters in the *Odyssey*—the Cyclops, the Chimaera, and others—and shows how Homer has portrayed these fantastic creatures in a strikingly realistic manner.]

The sources of the *Odyssey* are different from those of the *Iliad* and the difference explains some of its character. If it deals with marvels and monsters, so to a smaller extent does the *Iliad*. In both poems gods interfere with the course of nature. When Aphrodite spirits Paris away from the battlefield (*Iliad*, 3.380) or protects Aeneas (*Iliad*, 5.315–17), it is not very different from when Athene covers Odysseus with a mist in Phaeacia (7.15) or changes his appearance to prevent him being recognized (13.430–33). Though the *Iliad* contains the remarkable scene when the horse of Achilles speaks to him, it is because Hera has for this one occasion given it a human voice (*Iliad*, 19.40ff.), and this is well within the power of the gods. The *Odyssey* differs when its marvels are not caused by the gods but belong to the world of legend. The wind bag of Aeolus, the transformations of Circe, the summoning of ghosts at the end of the world, the monstrosity of Scylla are outside human experience and do not belong to the strictly heroic world of the *Iliad*. In face of them Odysseus conducts himself heroically, as when he insists on hearing the Sirens' song but forestalls disaster by getting himself lashed to the mast (12.178–79). But the monsters which he has to face are outside both human and heroic experience.

Homer evidently saw this and tried to bring his monsters as near as possible to humanity, to relate them to it, and even in some degree to humanize them. This is certainly the case with the Cyclops, who despite his single eye, his bulk "like a wooded peak of tall mountains" (9.190–92), and his cannibalistic gluttony, is made real by his pastoral life, by his care for his flocks, by his affection for his ram. He is hideous and horrible, but not outside comprehension. Comparable in some respects to him is the queen of the Laestrygonians. She lives in a rocky fjord, and all looks easy until the scouts of Odysseus entering her palace, "saw a woman as big as a mountain-peak, and they hated her" (10.113). She grabs one of them and plans to make her supper of him. She is of the same loathsome breed as the

Cyclops, but since he has recently received full treatment, she is deftly conveyed in a short sketch. The Sirens, despite their gift of song which lures men to death and the bones of decaying bodies round them (12.45–46), are careful to do no more than invite Odysseus to listen to them on the latest subjects of song (12.184–92). The exception to this realism is Scylla, who is a monster among monsters, aptly and fully described, with her twelve feet, her six necks, each with a head and three rows of teeth (12.89–91); she seizes six men from the ship of Odysseus and eats them while they are still crying for help and stretching out their hands, so that Odysseus comments:

> "That was the most piteous thing that I saw with my eyes of all that I suffered searching out the ways of the sea." (12.258–59)

Scylla must be descended from tales of sea monsters, of giant krakens and man-slaying cuttlefish, and perhaps because she has some basis in fact Homer feels that he must describe her exactly. She is far from ordinary, and yet one small touch brings her into the compass of living things—her voice is like that of a puppy (12.86). It is quite unexpected and almost absurd, and it is just this that brings it home. The monsters of the *Odyssey* are clearly visualized. Their horror comes not from vagueness but from clearly imagined actions and the menace of a horrible death which they offer. The only approximation to them in the *Iliad* is the Chimaera:

> It was a divine creature, not of human race, in front a lion, in the rear a snake, and in the middle a goat, and it breathed the terrible strength of flaming fire. (*Iliad*, 6.180–82)

Description is reduced to the barest essentials, but the Chimaera emerges clearly. This is the Homeric way of looking at monsters, and it is fully developed in the *Odyssey*. It is quite different from the shapeless horrors which the long northern night gives to its dragons.

—C. M. Bowra, "*The Odyssey:* Its Shape and Character," *Homer* (New York: Scribner's, 1972), pp. 133–34

[John H. Finley, Jr. (1904–1995) is the author of *Thucydides* (1942), *Pindar and Aeschylus* (1955), *Four Stages of Greek Thought* (1966), and *Homer's* Odyssey (1978), from which this extract is taken. Here, Finley examines Odysseus' descent into the Underworld, showing how his various encounters with the spirits of the dead both sum up his past adventures and prefigure his future ones.]

Over and above the guidance to his future that Odysseus gains in the Underworld, the poet intends it to show the nature of things, which the travels also show but less schematically. Judgment of the dead can hardly be absent. The sinners are not common men; their affront was against that Olympian rule the origin and existence of which Hesiod celebrates. Minos, a son of Zeus, is here the judge from whom souls hear their portion (11.568–571). The giant huntsman Orion, mentioned earlier with the sons of the heroine Iphimedeia who would have piled Pelion on Ossa, named also by Calypso among the mortal lovers whom the gods will not let goddesses keep—he was loved by the Dawn and killed by chaste Artemis on Ortygia (5.121–124)—still hunts in the asphodel meadow. His fate refutes Calypso's offer to Odysseus of agelessness and immortality. The still huger Tityus, son of Earth, lies outstretched, his liver feasted on by vultures as in ⟨Hesiod's⟩ *Theogony* (523–524) is Prometheus' liver by an eagle, because he laid hands on Leto. The liver is the seat of the passions; the eagle that afflicts Prometheus more directly expresses Zeus's anger, but Tityus attacked a bride of Zeus and, like Typhoeus the last rebel of the *Theogony,* is a son of Earth. Only the punishments of Tantalus and Sisyphus are described, their offenses being evidently taken as known. Tantalus stands in a pond, but the water dries and bare earth shows when he bends to drink; pears, pomegranates, apples, figs, and olives hang above him, but winds blow them skyward when he reaches to eat (11.582–592). Later myth had the gods share with him their nectar and ambrosia, which he stole to give to mortals (Pindar, *Ol.* 1.59–64). Sisyphus strains with arms and feet pushing a great rock toward a summit, just as it reaches which the shameless rock falls back and he repeats; sweat pours from him and dust is on his head (11.593–600). To Theognis (699–718) he is the clever man who tried to escape Hades; his cleverness is mentioned in the *Iliad* (6.153). These sinners, it was argued, finish the frame around the Trojan figures which the heroines initiate. The two groups jointly set the recent between the long past and shed example on it. There seems further tie to Hesiod in his distinguishing the beneficent earth-abiding spirits of the Golden Age from the flagitious subterranean spirits of the Silver Age and both from the demigods on the blessed isles. The tie is not of substance but of method and purpose. Though the sinners and the heroines have been thought later additions, they enlarge Odysseus' sight by the epic method of exemplary categories.

Heracles at the end like Anticleia at the start marvels at his mortal fate of gazing on the dead; the adventure rounds to a close. He too, he says, by fated service to a lesser man lived a life of endless labor, the extreme of which was descent to capture Cerberus. Yet, as with Odysseus, Hermes' and Athene's guidance let him do even that (11.625–626). The poem and the speech at Scheria start as tales of toil; the endurance that underlies the hero's many traits has its prototype in Heracles. He is such in *Iliad* 19 (95–125), though less for his labors than for the blindness by which Zeus himself was tricked by Hera to subjugate him to his inferior half-brother Eurystheus. Odysseus has now seen and endured more than fits a mortal, and the cry of the innumerable dead will soon speed him away. But his labors will end well, and that too is shown in Heracles, only whose shade appears in Hades while he himself takes joy among the gods with Hebe for wife (11.602–604). The explanation resembles that by which Odysseus later knows of Helius' anger for his slaughtered cattle. The motive is evident. Heracles was beyond others dear to his father Zeus; in the *Theogony* (529–531) he is for that reason given the fame of shooting the eagle and freeing Prometheus. Though his final translation to Olympus is first mentioned in the *Odyssey*, it is in the spirit of the poem as showing both release from toil and Zeus's final justice. His baldric, adorned with pictured animals and battles, resembles the crown that the *Theogony* Hephaestus makes for Pandora (11.610–612, *Theog.*

581–582). The themes by which the poet shows Odysseus can change fast; thus just earlier he told Alcinous that he would stay a year for greater gain, yet on the next afternoon he yearns like a tired laborer for sunset. The labor of his journey shows in Heracles, yet as the great ghost leaves and Persephone is about to rouse the screaming nations of the dead, Odysseus says that he waited in hope of speaking with other heroes. Labor and knowledge, the two themes that mark him at the start continue to describe him. Their interworking will make possible the return and peaceful end of which he learns in the Underworld, even as he learns the nature of the longer human history within which his famous life takes place. The travels chiefly show the natural world, Hades chiefly the world of history and example. The poet chose the story over many possible others, and it may tell something of him that, though possessed of these two forms of knowledge, the hero reaches home a beggar.

—John H. Finley, Jr., *Homer's* Odyssey (Cambridge, MA: Harvard University Press, 1978), pp. 126–28

JASPER GRIFFIN ON THE WOMEN IN THE *ODYSSEY*

[Jasper Griffin, Professor of Classical Languages and Literature at Balliol College, Oxford, is the author of *Homer* (1980), *Latin Poets and Roman Life* (1985), and *The Mirror of Myth* (1986). In this extract, Griffin compares three women in the *Odyssey*—Calypso, Circe, and Nausicaa—showing how each of them represents a type of woman for whom Odysseus might easily have abandoned his wife and his quest to return home.]

Odysseus is entertained and loved by two goddesses, Calypso and Circe, and he has to detach himself from each of them and also to say farewell to Nausicaa. With the glamorous Circe Odysseus happily spends a year in pleasure, 'feasting on meat inexhaustible and sweet wine'. Eventually his crew urge on him that it is time to go, and he embraces her knees in supplication, begging her to let him depart: his men are melting his heart with their lamentations, when she is not there to see. At once she answers: 'Son of Laertes, sprung from Zeus, Odysseus of the many wiles, do not remain longer in my house against your will . . .' Forthwith she plans their departure.

Very different is the loving Calypso. For seven years Odysseus has been kept prisoner on her island, without means of escape; she wishes to marry him and make him immortal, but he will have none of it. Day after day he sits gazing out to sea and weeping. At last the gods intervene and send Hermes to tell Calypso that she must let him go home. She pours out her feelings to Hermes in bitterness against the gods; then she finds Odysseus and tells him that he can go, if he will, 'for I shall send you off with all my heart.' The hero is naturally astonished, and she reassures him with a smile, saying 'My mind is righteous and my heart within me is not of iron; no, it is kindly.' The pair have a last interview, recorded with great delicacy and charm. She asks if he is really so anxious to see his wife, 'for whom you yearn every day', and suggests that she, as a goddess, must be far better-looking. The tactful Odysseus at once admits that Penelope is inferior in beauty but says, 'Yet even so I wish and long every day to come home . . .' Calypso never tells him why she lets him go, and Odysseus never knows; she claims the credit for her own soft heart, and in his presence only hints at her bitterness and the real reason when she says 'I shall send a favourable wind for you, so that you may reach your homeland in safety—if that is the will of the gods in heaven, who are stronger than I to devise and to carry out.' We see through these words her expression of the fact that, were it not for the gods, she would not be letting him go; but for Odysseus that meaning is lost.

Lastly, there is Nausicaa. The night before she meets Odysseus, she dreamt of getting married. When he appears, at first she does not find him impressive; but when he is bathed and glorified by Athena, she says to her maids, 'I wish that such a man might be called my husband, living here, and that he might be pleased to stay here!' She goes on to give a broad hint to Odysseus: 'If you come into town with me, malicious people will talk, saying "Who is this tall and handsome stranger with Nausicaa? Where did she find him? He will be her husband next."' And even her father seems to think the match an attractive one. But of course Odysseus is off home to his wife, and there is no place for Nausicaa. She does, however, manage to be in his way as he goes in to dinner and to have a last word with him. 'Farewell, stranger, and when you are in your homeland think sometimes of me and remember that to me first you owe the saving of your life.' Odysseus replies that if he returns home safely, 'There I shall honour you like a god all my days, for you rescued me, princess.' Three scenes of parting, each of them coloured by love, and all very different.

The situation of parting with a woman in love is an emotional and difficult one, which is calculated to bring out the real nature of both parties. It was to have a great future in literature. Virgil's Dido and the *Heroides* of Ovid are among its forms. The variants on the theme in the *Odyssey* show us three very different women: the hard-boiled Circe, to whom the affair has been one of pleasure which there is no point in trying to prolong; the young Nausicaa, with whom nothing is put into words and yet everything is there, in essence rather than in actuality; and the suffering Calypso, retaining her dignity as she loses her love. Each represents a type and offers a different relationship, to which the wandering hero might have abandoned himself, forgetting his wife and home. That he resists them all brings out his unconquerable resolution, the central fact of the *Odyssey*. But we observe also two other things: these women are inscrutable, and they are complex.

—Jasper Griffin, *Homer on Life and Death* (Oxford: Clarendon Press, 1980), pp. 56–58

ITALO CALVINO ON ODYSSEUS AS A HOAXER

[Italo Calvino (1923–1985) was one of the most important Italian novelists of the century. Among his more celebrated novels are *Il visconte dimezzato* (1952; translated as *The Cloven Viscount*), *La cosmicomiche* (1965; translated as *Cosmicomics*), and *Le citta invisibili* (1972; translated as *Invisible Cities*). In this extract,

Calvino maintains that Odysseus is a prototypical hoaxer in his use of disguises and in the many tales he spins.]

In the collective unconscious, the prince in beggar's rags is proof that every beggar is in fact a prince who is the victim of a usurpation and must regain his realm. Ulysses or Robin Hood, kings or kings' sons or knightly aristocrats fallen on evil days, when they triumph over their enemies will restore a society of the just in which their true identity will be revealed.

But is it the same identity as before? It may be that the Ulysses who arrives in Ithaca as a poor beggar unrecognized by everyone is no longer the same person as the Ulysses who departed for Troy. It is no coincidence that he had once saved his life by pretending his name was Nobody. The only immediate and spontaneous recognition comes from his dog, Argos, as if the continuity of the individual could make itself manifest through signs perceptible only to an animal.

For the nurse the proof of his identity was the scar left him by a boar's tusk, for his wife the secret of the manufacture of their marriage bed out of the roots of an olive tree, and for his father a list of fruit trees. These signs have nothing regal about them; they put the hero on the level of a poacher, a carpenter, a gardener. To them are added the qualities of physical strength and pitiless aggressiveness toward his enemies, and, above all, the favor shown by the gods, which is what convinces Telemachus, if only by an act of faith.

In his turn, the unrecognizable Ulysses wakes up in Ithaca and does not recognize his own country: Athena has to intervene to assure him that Ithaca is really and truly Ithaca. In the second half of the *Odyssey* the identity crisis is general. Only the story assures us that the characters and places are the same characters and places; but even the story changes. The tale that the unrecognizable Ulysses tells the shepherd Eumaeus, then his rival Antinoüs, and even Penelope, is another and completely different *Odyssey:* the wanderings that have brought the fictitious person whom he claims to be all the way there from Crete, a story far more likely than the one he himself had told to the king of the Phaeacians. Who is to say that this is not the "real" *Odyssey?* But this new *Odyssey* refers to yet another

Odyssey, for in his travels the Cretan had come across Ulysses. So here we have Ulysses speaking of a Ulysses traveling in countries where the "real" Ulysses never set foot.

That Ulysses is a hoaxer is already known before the *Odyssey.* Wasn't it he who thought up the great swindle of the wooden horse? And at the beginning of the *Odyssey* the first recollections of his character are two flashbacks to the Trojan War, told to each other consecutively by Helen and Menelaus. Two tales of trickery. In the first he disguises himself in order to enter the besieged city and wreak havoc; in the second he is shut up inside the wooden horse with his colleagues, and is able to prevent Helen from unmasking them by inducing them to talk.

In both these episodes Ulysses is associated with Helen—in the first she is an ally and an accomplice in his trick, in the second an adversary, who imitates the voices of the Achaeans' wives to tempt them to betray themselves. The role of Helen seems contradictory, but it is always marked by trickery. In the same way, Penelope's web is a stratagem symmetrical with that of the Trojan Horse, and like the latter is a product of manual dexterity and counterfeiting, so that the two main characteristics of Ulysses are also those of Penelope.

If Ulysses is a hoaxer, the entire account he gives to the king of the Phaeacians might be a pack of lies. In fact, these seagoing adventures of his, concentrated in four central books of the *Odyssey,* a rapid series of encounters with fantastic beings (the ogre Polyphemus, the winds bottled up in a wineskin, the enchantments of Circe, sirens and sea monsters), clash with the rest of the poem, which is dominated by grave tones, psychological tension, and a dramatic crescendo gravitating toward an end: the reconquest of his kingdom and of his wife besieged by suitors. Here, too, we find motifs in common with folk tales, such as Penelope's web and the test of drawing the bow, but we are on ground far closer to modern criteria of realism and likelihood. Supernatural interventions are concerned solely with the appearance of the Olympian gods, usually concealed in human forms.

We should remember, however, that the same adventures (especially the one with Polyphemus) are mentioned elsewhere in the poem, so that Homer confirms them. Not only that: the gods themselves discuss them on Olympus. And Menelaus also recounts an adventure of the same folk-tale stamp, his encounter with the Old Man of the Sea. We can only attribute these excursions into the realm of fantasy to a montage of traditions of diverse origins, handed down by bards and meeting up later in the Homeric *Odyssey,* which in the account given by Ulysses in the first person probably reveals its most archaic stratum.

—Italo Calvino, "The Odysseys within the *Odyssey*" (1981), *The Uses of Literature,* tr. Patrick Creagh (San Diego: Harcourt Brace Jovanovich, 1986), pp. 140–43

Sheila Murnaghan on Odysseus in Disguise

[Sheila Murnaghan is a professor of classics at the University of Pennsylvania and the author of *Disguise and Recognition in the* Odyssey (1987), from which the following extract is taken. Here, Murnaghan studies the symbolism of Odysseus' return to Ithaca in disguise, showing that this use of disguise makes the *Odyssey* simultaneously realistic and fantastic.]

The story that the *Odyssey* tells of its hero's disguised return serves as a medium for holding two contrasting visions in suspense. One is a vision of the difficulties and limitations of human life. It is eloquently expressed by Odysseus when he is in disguise, especially in his warning to Amphinomus; it is embodied in the hardluck stories that make up Odysseus' false tales and the biography of Eumaeus; it is voiced by Penelope in her expressions of despair; and it is exemplified in the world of the *Telemachy,* a world of valued but also ordinary social rituals, in which all the excitement is found in stories of the past, and in which legendary heroes appear in a diminished light. The harshness of this vision is tempered by its celebration of the various means through which these hardships can be alleviated or contained: social institutions, the continuity of the gen-

73

erations, the adaptability of the human heart, the vicarious pleasures of song.

The other is a vision that treats all of these realities as a form of disguise, as a screen masking the true story, which is the heroic tale of Odysseus' glorious return. It answers the realism of the first vision with fantasy and wish-fulfillment. The interplay of these two visions creates the *Odyssey*'s peculiar texture, which is at once more realistic and more fantastic than that of the *Iliad*. This opposition is cast into self-consciously literary terms in the *Odyssey* as it raises the question of which of its internal songlike narratives of Odysseus' experiences between Troy and his return to civilization is the true one, the romantic version told to the Phaeacians, or the realistic version found in Odysseus' Ithacan tales.

Through its accommodation of these two visions, the *Odyssey* represents two avenues to happiness, one that is anomalous and miraculous and one that is within the range of what can reasonably be hoped for in human life. But in the end, the poem does not give these solutions equal weight. The exigencies of narration—the need to present one event as following another and to arrive eventually at a conclusion—also allow for the establishment of hierarchies among divergent possibilities. In the logic embodied in the *Odyssey*'s plot, disguise is not only the opposite to recognition, it is also its prelude. Eventually Odysseus' disguise, with all that it signifies, gives way to his recognition. This recognition is certainly qualified by its dependence on factors that it would seem to deny: Telemachus' new-found self-sufficiency, Penelope's inability to hold out any longer, the fortuitous circumstance that Odysseus is there to convert her gesture of despair into the means of his triumph, but it is nonetheless the definitive conclusion to the *Odyssey*'s plot. Telemachus steps aside as master of the house to allow for the revelation of Odysseus' return, Penelope's reluctant attempt to replace Odysseus becomes a means of bringing him back, her guest becomes her husband, the past is restored in the present, and Odysseus' unique achievement is finally secure.

—Sheila Murnaghan, *Disguise and Recognition in the* Odyssey (Princeton: Princeton University Press, 1987), pp. 178–80

George E. Dimock on the Cyclops Episode as a Folktale

[George E. Dimock (b. 1917) is Professor Emeritus of Classical Languages and Literatures at Smith College in Northampton, Massachusetts. He has translated Euripides' *Iphigeneia at Aulis* (1992; with W. S. Merwin) and written *The Unity of the* Odyssey (1989), from which this extract is taken. Here, Dimock studies the Cyclops episode and claims that it is an amalgam of several ancient folktales and folk motifs.]

Odysseus's adventure with the Kyklops has strong affinities with folktale: with one folktale and two unrelated folk motifs, to be exact, which all may be older than Homer. In the first, a one-eyed giant shepherd holds the hero and his companions captive in a cave. He cooks and eats some of his prisoners and then goes to sleep. The hero then heats the spit on which his comrades were cooked and blinds the giant. In the morning, when the giant opens the door to let his sheep out of the cave, the hero escapes by crawling out on all fours covered with a sheepskin or underneath a living sheep. Once outside he taunts the giant, and the giant, pretending reconciliation, throws him a ring or other object of value. No sooner does the hero put it on or take it in his hand than it begins to cry out, "Here I am," and the hero must cut off his finger or fingers before he can get rid of it and escape. To this well-constructed story Homer has added the "nobody" trick and the motif of making the monster drunk, which are very ill attested as folktale. He has obviously made other changes also.

For these variations the explanations are not far to seek; in fact, the way in which Homer adapts traditional material to his own purposes is nowhere clearer than in this tale of Polyphemos. The giant's name, Much Fame, was very likely Homer's choice. It relates not to anything in the generic story itself but rather to Homer's use of the tale as a figure for winning identity. The addition of the nobody trick obviously contributes to the same end. In the supposedly parallel folk motif the trickster almost always, if not invariably, calls himself not Nobody but Myself. The demon who is the usual enemy in this case is foiled when the only accusation he can make is "Myself did it." Could there be a clearer indication than this that Odysseus's explicit achievement of identity in this adventure is the product of Homer's own mind rather than of the tradition?

The second folk motif imported into the basic story, making the shepherd drunk, also has nothing to do with the traditional giant shepherd but is due rather to Homer's conception of the Kyklops as the embodiment of the uncivilized. So too is the use of an olive log instead of a spit as the instrument of blinding. The absence of metal puts the Kyklops at a lower cultural level, as does Homer's modification of the story according to which he eats his victims raw. More important, the log, explicitly a section of a mastlike pole, conduces to the nautical theme; at the same time, the fact that it is of olive wood suggests Odysseus's undying fertility, as we shall see when we compare it to the olive thicket in which he awoke on Scherie and to the rooted olive stump which forms one corner of his and Penelope's bed.

It is obvious too why Homer discarded the sequel (if he knew it) involving the talking ring or other magical gift in favor of Odysseus's voluntary proclamation of his own role in exacting the gods' justice. He is not the man to fall for a pretty bauble like the ring; he is also not the man to skulk nameless for fear of Poseidon's hostility, any more than he can endure to remain hidden with Kalypso.

The conception of shepherd-as-ogre seems especially appropriate when one considers the lonely, primitive life of the Mediterranean summer sheepsteading. When a Greek audience hears of the solitary cannibal Polyphemos with his cave-cum-stockade and his sheep pens, cheeses, and milk pails, it must find the account both particularly familiar and particularly hair-raising. Above and beyond this, it is interesting to see how Homer makes his own use of the pastoral aspect. Odysseus and his companions do nothing so simple as to crawl forth draped in sheepskins. Instead, for his companions Odysseus ties sheep together in threes with willow withes, then himself twines his fingers and feet in the wood of the lead ram's back and hangs beneath his belly, waiting for dawn and release. All this is in the highest degree impractical. I hope nobody whom hold in regard ever has the task of tying three sheep together with willow withes in a manner calculated to last more than five minutes, let alone to support a grown man beneath the middle sheep's stomach. Homer succeeds only moderately in gliding over this difficulty by not telling us that the men are tied underneath until somewhat later in the story. As for Odysseus, if his feet are hooked over the ram's back, as in the nature of things they must be, Polyphemos will inevitably discover him. Yet none of this is of the slightest consequence. We accept that Polyphemos may let his sheep out at any time; therefore Odysseus and his men must be constantly ready. We accept that Odysseus is incomparably more enduring than his men; therefore they need three sheep and a hammock apiece while he hangs beneath the leader of the flock by his own muscle; finally, we accept that everyone can hang on until dawn arrives. It all results in a marvelously suspenseful story, and I intend no witticism. Odysseus's preeminent ability to endure is probably not Homer's invention, but it took Homer to see, first, how that endurance suited the story of the Man of Pain who achieved the survival of his ghost and, second, how it could be shown to advantage in the story of the trickster and the one-eyed, man-eating shepherd.

The question arises, What is the relation of Homer's use of traditional folk motifs to what may be called his narrative thinking under the inspiration of the Muse? Certainty in such matters cannot be arrived at, but it is important to have as plausible a theory as possible. Ordinarily, folktale is marked off from serious reconstruction of the past by its unlimited tolerance for the fantastic. It would be hard, on the other hand, to draw a line between folktale and, say, sailors' yarns, of which there were surely a great number current in Homer's day, the Greek age of colonization. At the same time, much that sailors told was true, more was believed, and, particularly with increased knowledge of foreign parts, it all found its place in the fund of what was considered possible human experience. For Homer as he brooded on what happened to Odysseus during his ten years' absence after Troy's fall, the story of the one-eyed giant shepherd would float into his mind, tagged not "folktale" but simply "possible." One-eyed giant Kyklopes already existed in the epic tradition (cf. Hesiod *Theogony* 139–46), and Homer's sense of the appropriateness for Odysseus of an encounter with such a being surely overwhelmed the trivial difficulties of tying sheep together with withes or eluding Polyphemos's groping hands. The events of the folktale, or rather of Homer's revised version of it, were so appropriate that they must have happened to Odysseus, and therefore, guaranteed by the Muse, they did.

When Odysseus recounts the story to the Phaeacians, however, he has not yet achieved the survival of his ghost. On the one hand, his triumph was a great one: he successfully cast his name in the Kyklops's teeth, and he now knows that Poseidon will not kill him (5.341). When he rejoined the rest of his fleet, his men awarded him the ram in addition to his share of the booty, despite the loss of six men (9.550–51). The ram he promptly sacrificed to Zeus. Yet, as he relates it to the Phaeacians, the whole affair is clouded by hindsight.

> The ram on the beach
> to Zeus-of-the-Black-Clouds, son of Kronos, I sacrificed,
> and burned the thigh pieces; but he had no regard for my offering;
> he was pondering how all my ships with their beautiful benches
> would be lost, and my cherished companions.   (9.551–55)

Therefore it may be with foreboding rather than elation, and a good deal less than convinced of the value of city sacking, in spite of Odysseus's conquest of the Kyklops, that both the Phaeacians and we ourselves approach the events of the tenth book.

—George E. Dimock, *The Unity of the* Odyssey (Amherst: University of Massachusetts Press, 1989), pp. 116–18

NANCY FELSON-RUBIN ON PENELOPE

[Nancy Felson-Rubin is a professor of classics at the University of Georgia and the author of *Regarding Penelope* (1994), from which the following extract is taken. Here, Felson-Rubin focuses on the character of

Penelope, showing that it is she and not Odysseus who really overcomes the suitors.]

The suitors, like Agamemnon, misconstrue female power. They see it as victimizing and disempowering them, especially after they intercept Penelope unraveling Laertes' shroud; and they view the deceptive woman (Penelope) as a powerful menace, a siren, so to speak, who threatens their survival. Hence they bully her, in an effort to exercise some control. Then, like Agamemnon, they experience an untimely death—as they see it, at a woman's hand.

The suitors play an enabling role in the performance setting. Through them, various males in the audience can progress in their maturation journeys toward a more subtle attitude toward the female other. If we imagine a diverse live audience, made up (perhaps) of incorrigible "ranters" and "laggards" (lagging in their maturation process), we can then ask what each audience segment and what the audience in its totality might gain from watching the suitors meet their doom.

Clearly, the entire audience, of whatever age or gender, will gain confidence and solidarity from rebuking the villainous suitors and will experience relief at their destruction. Special beneficiaries are those listeners who identify, even temporarily, with the suitors' plight. Perhaps the easy, self-indulgent life-style of the suitors, as a band, ensnares them, as they recognize in the suitors' excesses traces of themselves: their indolence, their self-indulgence, their obtuseness about woman. By identifying with the suitors and by eventually disidentifying, these listeners—especially the laggards—can escape (in real life) the emotional traps that ensnare their fictional counterparts. No doubt, as they hear the epic unfold and come to regard the suitors as dangerous and beyond tolerance, these segments of the audience, identifying with Telemakhos, will disassociate from the suitors and even come to *desire* their demise. Indeed, to disavow the suitors is to disavow suitor-tendencies or suitor-elements in themselves. Thus the suitors, as characters, give these members of the audience a chance to grow and learn through abandoning their own suitor-qualities.

Naturally, characters inhabiting the same world as the suitors do not enjoy the luxury of reviling the suitors from a distance;

the danger is too near at hand. These include Telemakhos, Penelope, Odysseus, Athena as Mentes and Mentor, Eumaios, Philoitios, and Eurykleia. So Telemakhos, for example, might urge the suitors to leave the palace (1.374–75) and pray that they may perish for their crimes (1.378–80), while Athena-Mentes prays that Odysseus will return in time to dispatch them (1.265–66, echoed by Menelaos at 4.345–46). The cumulative effect of such exhortations and prayers is to kindle the listeners' desire that the crime and punishment story end in the suitors' slaughter. This impulse for closure must outweigh any good-natured, self-indulgent attachments listeners have formed to one villainous suitor or another.

The evaluation of the suitors by various characters in the text and especially by segments of the live audience fluctuates as the epic unfolds. Neither the suitors nor Penelope can hold a fixed position in the moral hierarchy: now one element, now the other claims audience sympathy or disapproval. Indeed, the evaluation of Penelope is inversely proportionate to that of her suitors; as she fares well, they sink, and vice versa. Though Penelope triumphs in the end, at certain junctures the suitors enjoy audience sympathy and regard; they voice such strong opinions that, through their eyes, the audience sees the Ithakan queen as both a materfamilias and an alluring, dangerous enchantress, a siren.

The slaughter of the suitors, the cleansing of the palace, and the truce with the relatives provide aesthetic closure to the *Odyssey*. These events, like the brutal hanging of the maidservants, appear to eliminate every moral ambiguity and, together, to streamline the plot. Yet to the extent that the lives of individual suitors could have ended differently, the "final solution" in the *Odyssey* remains open to scrutiny. As in the case of Penelope, whose alternative plot possibilities are kept alive up until 23.205–6, so with the suitors: despite all the signals for the inevitability of their death, alternative pathways their lives might have taken are raised as possibilities, presumably stirring hope and desire in segments of the audience that one or the other of the suitors will reform his ways in time. ⟨. . .⟩

The suitors are no match for Penelope. Her wiliness is more than they can handle. They are her inferiors in age and insight and, as such, they naturally and inevitably become her victims, casualties in her story of reunion with Odysseus. They perish through their own moral blindness, bringing about their own demise, but also through their inability to interact with Penelope. This is the dominant view of Homer and of most characters in the text. From their own angle and perspective, however, as expressed most definitively by Amphimedon's shade (24.125–90), Penelope had a strong hand in their destruction. First, she never intended to marry one of them; she devised the ruse of the shroud to thwart their suit. Second, she helped contrive their slaughter, planning it along with her husband. Between her first deceit and their demise, they did behave reprehensibly, but only because she kept stringing them along. That is why they became her victims, slaughtered by her husband in the contest of the bow.

Homer lessens the suitors' automatic blameworthiness by diverse ploys. First, he paints them as immature and unschooled, as well as intrinsically flawed. He individualizes them, so that some seem more salvageable and less reprehensible than others. All are aristocrats, from the best families. One (Amphinomos) gets a temporary window of escape; another (Eurymakhos) a quasi-heroic death. Then, too, Homer partially exonerates them by making a few respectable characters blame society for indulging these youths and tolerating their misbehavior. Finally, we can infer that, in the past, before they discovered Penelope unraveling Laertes' shroud by night and before Telemakhos had come of age, the suitors were less violent and better mannered; at that time, they had more cordial relations with Telemakhos, who dined with them, and perhaps with Penelope; hence they must possess an intrinsic humanity.

—Nancy Felson-Rubin, *Regarding Penelope: From Character to Poetics* (Princeton: Princeton University Press, 1994), pp. 109–11

CHARLES SEGAL ON DEATH AND REBIRTH IN THE *ODYSSEY*

[Charles Segal (b. 1936) was for many years a professor of classics at Brown University before becoming a professor of classics and comparative literature at Princeton University. He has written many books, including *Tragedy and Civilization: An Interpretation of Sophocles* (1981), *Pindar's Mythmaking* (1986), and *Lucretius on Death and Anxiety* (1990). In this extract, taken from a book on the *Odyssey* that gathers together in revised form several of his earlier essays, Segal maintains that the pattern of death and rebirth is an important ritualistic element that structures the entire poem.]

Birth and death, then, the most mysterious passages of human life, underlie the overall rhythm of the return and oscillate ambiguously in it in a kind of contrapuntal movement. To obtain passage back to mortal life, Odysseus must visit the land of the dead. The knowledge of his own death gained from this visit is present to him even at the moment of the joyful reclaiming of his human life and his spouse: "O wife, we have not yet come to the limit of our trials, but afterward there will be still measureless toil, much and difficult," he begins (23.248), and goes on to tell her, reluctantly, of Teiresias' prophecy of his death (263–84). Earlier, Odysseus regarded his Phaeacian landing as a rebirth and thanked Nausicaa for "giving him life" (8.468). It is fitting that the fresh princess should be the restorer of life to the exhausted warrior; yet his sleep on the ship that brings him back to the mortal world and fulfills the Phaeacians' promise is "most like to death" (13.80). In the same contrapuntal fashion, the dead suitors are paraded off by Hermes, "leader of souls" (*psuchagōgos* or *psuchopompos*) as the grim counterpart to Odysseus' successful return to full "life."

Odysseus' rebirth is also a source of life for those who waited: son, wife, and father. It is a rebirth for Odysseus' line as well, marked in the joyful utterance of Laertes, himself rejuvenated after his bath (24.365–82), when he sees "son and grandson striving concerning excellence" (24.515). The renewal of Odysseus' life is here fulfilled in terms beyond himself and he stands in the middle as the link between generations, between past and future. This rebirth is transferred also into moral and social terms at the very end of the *Odyssey*: the interference of the gods ends the cycle of strife and assures "wealth and peace in abundance," as Zeus had promised Athena (24.486). The poem thus ends with the order of Zeus with which it began; and the promised restoration of the land comes with the return of the rightful king and "gentle father," as foreshadowed in Odysseus' first words with Penelope on his return, when he addresses her, disguised as a beggar, in the darkened halls:

> My lady, never a man in the wide world
> should have a fault to find with you. Your name
> has gone out under heaven like the sweet
> honor of some god-fearing king, who rules
> in equity over the strong: his black lands bear
> both wheat and barley, fruit trees laden bright,
> new lambs at lambing time—and the deep sea
> gives great hauls of fish by his good strategy,
> so that his folk fare well.   (19.107–14; Fitzgerald's translation)

Though Penelope and Odysseus have not yet explicitly recognized each other, they meet here both as the individual characters they are and as the archetypal king and queen, the partners in a sacred marriage. In terms of Frye's "encyclopedic range" of epic, their union symbolizes the ever-renewed fertility of the earth and the fruitful harmony between society and cosmos.

These ritual elements not only imply this larger dimension of meaning but also point to an artistic function behind a basic component of the poem's style: the ritualizing quality of the repeated formulas. Through the repetition of the verbal formulas, the recurrent acts of sleep, bathing, entrance, and departure stand out in a suggestive ritual character, with the overtones of meaning carried by that ritual character for a society such as Homer's. One may regard this cooperation of matter and style as a happy by-product of Homeric language. Yet there may be an inner congruence between the material and the style, a congruence that grows out of the culture itself and its means of apprehending and ordering the world. The outwardly inflexible demands of the oral style, in other words, seem to suit the ritual modes of thought that doubtless helped to create the style in the first place. These are modes of thought in which recurrent cycles of loss and regeneration, alienation and rediscovery, and death and rebirth are celebrated as the fundamental facts of existence and form an organic link between human life and the natural world. Such cyclical patterns are both metaphor and reality; and the ritual patterns discussed here help unite the two, for ritual itself partakes of both play and seriousness, both imaginary projection and realistic confrontation.

The very fabric of Homer's language, then, presents the expected, reenacted situations that make up the return through the equally predictable, crystallized, ritualized expressions that make up the formulas. These recurrent formulaic expressions themselves intimate the steady sameness, the shared narrowness, and the richness in limitation that form the substance of that for which the hero has journeyed back to Ithaca. The contrast between the circumscribed, formulaic language of the *Odyssey* and the richly varied, brightly colored adventures it describes also reflects the poem's movement between exploration and return, between the exotic and the familiar, and between the open possibilities of the free traveler who consorts with goddesses and the accepted constraints and rewards of the land dweller who is bound to a mortal woman.

—Charles Segal, *Singers, Heroes, and Gods in the* Odyssey (Ithaca, NY: Cornell University Press, 1994), pp. 82–84

Books by
Homer

Greek text:

Opera. Ed. Demetrios Chalkokondyles. 1489.

Odysseia. Ed. Aldo Pio Manuzio. 1504.

[*Works.*] Ed. Jacobus Micyllus and Joachim Camerarius. 1541.

Opera. Ed. Samuel Clarke. 1729–40. 4 vols.

[*Works.*] Ed. Thomas Grenville, Richard Porson, et al. 1800.
4 vols. in 2.

[*Works.*] Ed. Wilhelm Dindorf. 1824–28. 3 vols. in 2.

Odyssey. Ed. Henry Hayman. 1866–82. 3 vols.

Odyssea. Ed. Arthur Ludwich. 1890. 2 vols. in 1.

Opera. Ed. David B. Monro and Thomas W. Allen. 1902–12.
5 vols.

Odyssey. Ed. A. T. Murray. 1919. 2 vols.

L'Odyssée. Ed. Victor Bérard. 1924–25. 3 vols.

Odyssey. Ed. W. B. Stanford. 1947–48. 2 vols.

Odyssea. Ed. Helmut van Thiel. 1991.

English translations:

The Whole Works of Homer. Tr. George Chapman. 1616.

The Travels of Ulysses. Tr. Thomas Hobbes. 1673.

The Odyssey of Homer. 1725–26. 5 vols.

The Iliad and Odyssey of Homer. Tr. William Cowper. 1791.
   2 vols.

The Odyssey of Homer. Tr. William Cullen Bryant. 1871. 2 vols.
   in 1.

The Odyssey of Homer. Tr. S. H. Butcher and Andrew Lang.
   1879.

The Odyssey of Homer. Tr. William Morris. 1887. 2 vols.

The Odyssey. Tr. Samuel Butler. 1900.

The Odyssey of Homer. Tr. T. E. Shaw [T. E. Lawrence]. 1932.

The Story of Odysseus. Tr. W. H. D. Rouse. 1937.

The Odyssey. Tr. E. V. Rieu. 1945.

The Odyssey. Tr. Robert Fitzgerald. 1961.

The Odyssey. Tr. Albert Cook. 1967.

The Odyssey of Homer. Tr. Richmond Lattimore. 1967.

The Odyssey of Homer. Tr. Allen Mandelbaum. 1990.

Works about Homer and the *Odyssey*

Abrahamson, Ernest. *The Adventure of Odysseus.* St. Louis: Washington University Press, 1960.

Amory, Anne. "The Gates of Horn and Ivory." *Yale Classical Studies* 20 (1966): 3–57.

Austin, Norman. *Archery at the Dark of the Moon: Poetic Problems in Homer's* Odyssey. Berkeley: University of California Press, 1975.

Belmont, David E. "Twentieth-Century Odysseus." *Classical Journal* 62 (1966): 49–56.

Beye, Charles R. *The* Iliad, *the* Odyssey, *and the Epic Tradition.* Garden City, NY: Doubleday/Anchor, 1966.

Bloom, Harold, ed. *Homer's* The Odyssey. New York: Chelsea House, 1988.

———, ed. *Odysseus/Ulysses.* New York: Chelsea House, 1991.

Boitani, Piero. *The Shadow of Ulysses: Figures of a Myth.* Tr. Anita Weston. Oxford: Clarendon Press, 1994.

Bradford, Ernie. *Ulysses Found.* London: Hodder & Stoughton, 1963.

Brown, Calvin S. "Odysseus and Polyphemus: The Name and the Curse." *Comparative Literature* 18 (1966): 193–202.

Camps, W. A. *An Introduction to Homer.* Oxford: Clarendon Press, 1980.

Carpenter, Rhys. *Folktale, Fiction and Saga in the Homeric Epics.* Berkeley: University of California Press, 1946.

Clarke, Howard W. *The Art of the* Odyssey. Englewood Cliffs, NJ: Prentice-Hall, 1967.

Clay, Jenny Strauss. *The Wrath of Athena: Gods and Men in the* Odyssey. Princeton: Princeton University Press, 1983.

Dietrich, B. C. *Death, Fate and the Gods.* London: Athlone Press, 1965.

Dimock, George. "Crime and Punishment in the *Odyssey.*" *Yale Review* 60 (1971): 199–214.

Else, G. E. *Homer and the Homeric Problem.* Cincinnati: University of Cincinnati Press, 1965.

Farron, S. G. "The *Odyssey* as an Anti-Aristocratic Statement." *Studies in Antiquity* 1 (1979–80): 59–101.

Fenik, Bernard. *Studies in the* Odyssey. Wiesbaden: Franz Steiner, 1974.

———, ed. *Homer: Tradition and Invention.* Leiden: E. J. Brill, 1978.

Flaumenhaft, Mera J. "The Undercover Hero: Odysseus from Dark to Daylight." *Interpretation* 10 (1982): 9–41.

Foley, Helene P. " 'Reverse Similes' and Sex Roles in the *Odyssey.*" *Arethusa* 11 (1978): 7–26.

Frame, Douglas. *The Myth of Return in Early Greek Epic.* New Haven: Yale University Press, 1978.

Gray, Wallace. *Homer to Joyce.* New York: Macmillan, 1985.

Hansen, William F. *The Conference Sequence.* Berkeley: University of California Press, 1972.

Harrison, E. L. "Notes on Homeric Psychology." *Phoenix* 14 (1960): 63–80.

Heatherington, M. E. "Chaos, Order, and Cunning in the *Odyssey.*" *Studies in Philology* 73 (1976): 225–38.

Hogan, J. C. "The Temptation of Odysseus." *Proceedings of the American Philological Association* 106 (1976): 187–210.

Kearns, Emily. "The Return of Odysseus: A Homeric Theoxeny." *Critical Quarterly* 32 (1982): 2–8.

Kirk, G. S. *Homer and the Oral Tradition.* Cambridge: Cambridge University Press, 1978.

──────. *The Language and Background of Homer.* Cambridge: Cambridge University Press, 1964.

Kitto, H. D. F. "The *Odyssey*." In Kitto's *Poiesis: Structure and Thought.* Berkeley: University of California Press, 1966, pp. 116–52.

Knight, W. F. Jackson. *Many-Minded Homer: An Introduction.* Ed. John D. Christie. London: George Allen & Unwin, 1968.

Lord, A. B. *The Singer of Tales.* Cambridge, MA: Harvard University Press, 1960.

Mahaffy, J. P. "The Degradation of Odysseus in Greek Literature." *Hermathena* 1 (1874): 265–75.

Newton, Rick M. "The Rebirth of Odysseus." *Greek, Roman, and Byzantine Studies* 25 (1984): 5–20.

Page, Denys. *Folktales in Homer's* Odyssey. Cambridge, MA: Harvard University Press, 1973.

Parry, Adam. *The Homeric* Odyssey. Oxford: Clarendon Press, 1955.

Parry, Milman. *The Making of Homeric Verse.* Oxford: Oxford University Press, 1971.

Phillips, E. D. "Odysseus in Italy." *Journal of Hellenic Studies* 73 (1953): 53–67.

Pocock, L. G. *Odyssean Essays.* Oxford: Basil Blackwell, 1965.

Powell, Barry B. *Composition by Theme in the* Odyssey. Meisenheim am Glan: Verlag Anton Hain, 1977.

Pucci, Pietro. "The Song of the Sirens." *Arethusa* 12 (1979): 121–32.

Rose, Gilbert P. "The Swineherd and the Beggar." *Phoenix* 34 (1980): 285–97.

Rubino, Carl A., and Cynthia W. Shelmerdine, ed. *Approaches to Homer.* Austin: University of Texas Press, 1983.

Rutherford, R. B. "The Philosophy of the *Odyssey*." *Journal of Hellenic Studies* 106 (1986): 145–62.

Scully, Stephen. "Doubling in the Tale of Odysseus." *Classical World* 80 (1986–87): 401–17.

Seidel, Michael, and Edward Mendelson, ed. *Homer to Brecht: The European Epic and Dramatic Traditions.* New Haven: Yale University Press, 1977.

Skulsky, Harold. "Circe and Odysseus: Metamorphosis as Enchantment." In Skulsky's *Metamorphosis: The Mind in Exile.* Cambridge, MA: Harvard University Press, 1981, pp. 10–23.

Stanford, W. B. "The Ending of the *Odyssey:* An Ethical Approach." *Hermathena* 100 (1965): 5–20.

Stewart, Douglas. *The Disguised Guest: Rank, Role, and Identity in the* Odyssey. Lewisburg, PA: Bucknell University Press, 1976.

Taylor, Charles H., ed. *Essays on the* Odyssey. Bloomington: Indiana University Press, 1963.

Thornton, Agathe. *People and Themes in Homer's* Odyssey. London: Methuen, 1970.

Vivante, Paolo. *The Homeric Imagination.* Bloomington: Indiana University Press, 1970.

–––––––. *Homer.* New Haven: Yale University Press, 1985.

Walcott, P. "Odysseus and the Art of Lying." *Ancient Society* 8 (1977): 1–19.

Woodhouse, W. J. *The Composition of Homer's* Odyssey. Oxford: Clarendon Press, 1929.

Index